Greg Lanier [...] this short bu[...] member both to understand the process of how we got our Bibles, and to have well-founded confidence in the text of God's word before us. An edifying and enlightening book in an age of fake news and false assertions on this foundational subject.

Lee Gatiss
Church Historian at Union School of Theology, and Director
of Church Society (UK)

If you are looking for a readable, informed, and theologically-grounded explanation for where our Bibles came from, then this new volume by Greg Lanier is it. Finally, we have an accessible book on the biblical canon that is answering the kind of questions ordinary Christians are asking. I highly recommend it.

Michael J. Kruger
President and Professor of New Testament, Reformed
Theological Seminary, Charlotte, North Carolina

This book is tailor-made for people like me—people who would say that their life is built around the Bible, yet would find it difficult to explain how the Bible came together, or to defend challenges to the Bible's trustworthiness. Without being overly wordy or technical, this pocket guide provides clear and accessible explanations for why we can be confident that our Bibles are the Word of God.

Nancy Guthrie
Author and Bible Teacher

Carefully researched and easy to read, Greg Lanier has provided an excellent resource for both pastors and laypeople. Beginning with a definition of scripture as 'the inspired deposit of writings received as divinely authoritative for the covenant community,' Dr. Lanier takes his reader through the history and complexity of our Bible. This pocket guide answers difficult questions about the formation of the canon of scripture with clarity, precision, and a pastor's heart.

Leigh Swanson
First Presbyterian Church of Orlando, and VP of Community Development for Reformed Theological Seminary, Orlando, Florida

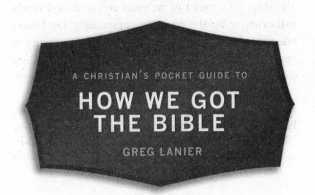

A CHRISTIAN'S POCKET GUIDE TO

HOW WE GOT
THE BIBLE

GREG LANIER

Old and New Testament Canon and Text

CHRISTIAN
FOCUS

Scripture quotations, unless otherwise indicated, are from
The Holy Bible, English Standard Version, copyright © 2001
by Crossway Bibles, a publishing ministry of Good News
Publishers. Used by permission. All rights reserved. esv Text
Edition: 2011.

Copyright © Greg Lanier 2018

paperback ISBN 978-1-5271-0268-2
epub ISBN 978-1-5271-0313-9
mobi ISBN 978-1-5271-0314-6

10 9 8 7 6 5 4 3 2 1

Published by Christian Focus Publications Ltd,
Geanies House, Fearn, Ross-shire,
IV20 1TW, Scotland, Great Britain
www.christianfocus.com

Cover design by Daniel Van Straaten
Printed and bound by Norhaven

To my church family.
May you always trust in the very
words of the living God.

CONTENTS

CONTENTS

⚠ Warning
✎ Don't Forget
⑦ Stop and Think
❋ Point of Interest

PREFACE

'Wait, what do you mean by First Maccabees?
I've never heard of that.'

'Pastor, where on earth is Acts 8:37?'

In recent weeks I was asked these questions by two long-time Christians who know their Bibles well and have spent time reading serious Christian literature. Yet their questions revealed a gap in knowledge that even mature Christians may have in terms of the formation of Scripture. What makes up the 'canon' and why? Why does my copy of the Bible not include certain verses that show up in others? Such questions, if handled poorly, can lead to a diminished confidence in Scripture. They are the stimulus for this book.

Without a doubt, dozens of books have been written on the topic of the origins and transmission of the Old and New Testaments. Why write another? This short volume aims to fill a particular gap. Most available volumes are intimidatingly long and technical, even for specialists. Some that are pitched more at the popular level can be frustratingly out-of-date or do not deal fairly or robustly with the data—giving the impression of 'hiding something.' The vast majority cover *only* the OT or *only* the NT, but not both. And many of the best have focused only on one aspect of these key questions, such as 'canon,' and not others.

My aim, then, is to prepare a volume that, say, my aunt or uncle would enjoy reading but which engages rigorously with the data, covers both testaments, and cogently covers the central aspects of the question, 'How did we get the Bible?'

The genesis of my interest in these issues goes back to my time as a layperson under the ministry of Dr. Michael Kruger, whom I'm now privileged to call a colleague at Reformed Theological Seminary. His influence and that of Dr. Charles Hill (another RTS colleague) loom large in the following pages, particularly for the New Testament. The materials and concepts that led to the present volume first took shape in seminars I have taught on the topic at Christ Church Cambridge (UK) and River Oaks Church (Florida), though the finer details have been worked out in my academic publications and courses on the Greek OT, Gospels, and Pauline Corpus.

The topics that will be covered are deemed, by some, to be rather dry. Haven't we sorted this stuff out already? However, time and again I have been approached by church members with insightful and probing questions about why their Bible mentions textual variants (are they hiding something from me?), or what to make of the apocrypha (is it dangerous?), or what to make of the latest *Time* article lambasting the trustworthiness of the Bible (is this stuff true?). For many Christians, the questions addressed by this volume are not just 'ivory tower' but very personal, for they want to know, at the end of the day, whether they can turn to their NIV or ESV or NKJV and trust that it is the Word of God.

Moreover, in recent decades both popular and academic writers have engaged in a sophisticated critique of the origins of the Bible, the nature of canon, and the reliability of the text we have today. Though such endeavors are by no means new, they are increasingly popularized on numerous fronts, from college religion courses to mainstream media to Islamic apologetics.

My goal, then, is not necessarily to win any big debates nor convince learned academicians to change their views. Rather, my hope in such a *Pocket Guide* is to provide the average interested Christian—using my own church as my theoretical audience—with a thoroughly Christian and academically sound (two things that do not often go together) resource, both for their own edification and for engaging with folks who might disagree with them on these matters. In the interest of full disclosure, I cannot help but offer a Protestant, and specifically Reformed, perspective on many of these issues, but my desire is that the volume be accessible and useful to the entire church catholic.

A DIVINE DEPOSIT

Few things are better suited for conspiracy theorists than the subject of the origins of the Bible.

Consider a few recent examples. Allegations of forged scrolls from Israel have brought suspicion on the 2017 opening of the Museum of the Bible in Washington D.C. The so-called 'Gospel of Jesus' Wife'—a papyrus fragment purporting to record Jesus' words to his 'wife'—brought intense international attention when published in 2012, only to be demonstrated a forgery in 2016. The *Gospel of Judas*, which offers a remix story of Judas Iscariot and Jesus, caused a media firestorm in 2006. And who can forget the salacious theories about repressed gospels and Constantine's canon power-play in Dan Brown's 2003 *The Da Vinci Code*. ?

Most everyone, it seems, loves a good conspiracy about Scripture, and questions raised about such important writings can be quite polarizing, if not emotional.

Are the Scriptures truly from God? If so, in what sense? If not, are they merely erroneous human devotional writings? Who picked which books are 'in' and 'out,' and how did *they* get to be the ones deciding? Was the canon foisted upon us by rabbis at Jamnia or bishops at Nicaea? And is it true, as many Muslims and academics claim, that the texts of these Scriptures are so polluted by errors that they are hopelessly corrupt?

These questions radiate from a central concern: *how did we get the Scriptures, and can I accept them as the Word of God?* I admit that the latter half of the question is not really the domain of human argumentation; it is an essential faith commitment. But we can perhaps make some headway on the former, helping the believer to develop a more well-articulated set of convictions, and the skeptic to take a fresh look at things.

GETTING OUR BEARINGS

We will break down our task into the three essential building blocks for understanding how the Scriptures got from their point of origin to today. First, we must ask the question, 'What exactly is Scripture in the first place?' Though this question often goes unasked, or receives a simplistic answer, it the foundational starting point and will be the topic of the rest of this chapter.

Second, 'Do we have the right *books*?' Since the two

testaments have different historical backgrounds, we will address them separately in chapters 2 and 4.

Third, 'Do we have the right *words* of these books?' Even if we are convinced we have the 'right' books, we also must spend time thinking through the complex process by which the words of those books were passed down both orally and via handwritten copies over a multi-century period before the printing press (and computers). Again we will address each testament individually, in chapters 3 and 5.

In sum, I will develop a brief case for *what Scripture is*, followed by a study on *canon* and *text* for the Old and New Testaments, respectively. Let us dig in.

WHAT IS SCRIPTURE?

Paul's words, 'when the old covenant is read' (2 Cor 3:14), seem innocent enough. They did to me, at least, until I realized the shocking implications of what he was saying. Here a minister of the 'new covenant' (2 Cor 3:6) makes a stunning claim that the 'old covenant'—referring to the relationship established by God by which he redeems a people unto himself in fulfillment of his promises— is *something to be read*. It is concretized in a book: a covenantal book. Here we have the seed of the answer to our question, 'What is Scripture?'

We begin here because articulating what Scripture *is* feeds into the other issues we will face, not the other way around. When the early Jewish and Christian communities discussed these matters, they did not start with agonizing decisions about 'canonization' to select books to be Scripture. They spoke of what they already deemed to be 'covenant,' 'writings,' 'holy books,' and 'books that defile the hands' (that is, sacred). They talked about what exactly it *is* that they had in front of them, and the answer to *that* question directed the downstream concerns about the shape of that *thing* and whether we have good copies of it. The food in a package determines what stats show up on the nutrition label and whether they are accurate, not the other way around. What the thing *is* anchors the rest of the discussion.

Attempting to define Scripture is, however, slightly terrifying and always debatable. That said, I propose that the most accurate and minimally sufficient way to define Scripture—biblically, theologically, and historically—is the following: it is *the inspired deposit of writings received as divinely authoritative for the covenant community*. Space does not permit going into extreme detail unpacking this, but I will do my best to elaborate briefly on what I mean for each element of the definition.

'INSPIRED'

Scripture bears witness to its own dual authorship: God himself, by the Holy Spirit, and the human authors who give particular expression in human language. This is traditionally called 'inspiration,' taking a cue from Paul's classic phrase in 2 Timothy 3:16a, 'all Scripture is God-breathed' (*theo* [God] + *pneustos* [breathed/inspired]). The OT is described as being inscribed by the 'finger of

God' (Exod 31:8), given by the 'voice of God' (Deut 13:18), delivered to Moses 'face to face' (Exod 33:11), and stamped with God's own authority as 'the Word of the LORD' or 'Word of God' (over 300x). Both testaments bear witness that they were given directly by the Spirit of God yet *through* human instruments (1 Kgs 16:34; Zech 7:12; Luke 1:70; 1 Pet 1:10–12).

Judaism has always viewed the Hebrew Scriptures as word-for-word given directly by God from heaven (*b. Sanh.* 11a). The same is true for the early church. For example, Clement of Alexandria (d. 215 AD) attests that John was 'inspired by the Spirit' to compose his Gospel (Eusebius, *Hist.* 6.14.5–7). The *Anti-Marcionite Prologue to Luke* (ca. 150–250 AD) likewise describes Luke as 'moved by the Holy Spirit [to] write down the gospel.'

It is helpful to further refine this view of divine/ human authorship by thinking of it as a three-legged stool. (i) *Verbal.* The historical orthodox church affirms that divine inspiration extends not just to the ideas contained in Scripture, but to the very words in the original languages (see Matt 5:18). (ii) *Plenary.* The church historically affirms that divine inspiration extends to *all the words*, including historical facts/figures, not just the words conveying 'spiritual' truths. (iii) *Organic.* Scripture is clear that the writers' minds/personalities, linguistic abilities, and cultural experiences were fully

The idea that scriptural writers were in a trance receiving divine dictation is more representative of a Muslim or Mormon view than the historical Christian teaching.

engaged. This 'organic' process is present everywhere—
i.e. diverse genres and styles of writing, interaction
with both biblical and non-biblical sources (Acts 17:28),
adaptation to historical circumstances (Jer 36)—but is
made particularly clear in Luke 1:1–4 ('having followed
things closely') and 1 Peter 1:10 ('searched and inquired
carefully'). The Spirit perfectly superintended their full
faculties as writers.

'Inspired,' in a nutshell, is simply this: 'men spoke
from God as they were carried along by the Holy Spirit'
(2 Pet 2:21). An important follow-on question often
arises. Did the writers *know* they were writing 'inspired
Scripture'? Of course, we cannot probe their psyches
from available sources. However, numerous lines of
evidence indicate that the authors indeed knew what
they were doing.

On the OT side, the writers constantly indicate that
they are communicating nothing less than 'Thus says
the LORD' (over 600x). Even the writers of poetic books
indicate via superscriptions, *selah*, and other instructions
that their compositions are designed for worship.

On the NT side, the primary writers were directly
authorized by Jesus to be his 'witnesses' (Matt. 10:1–4, 40;
Luke 24:48–49; John 20:21–23; Acts 1:8). Though none
say explicitly, 'I'm writing inspired covenantal Scriptures'
(would have been nice if they had!), there are plenty
of indicators of this self-awareness. They were not
just catching up with friends. The apostolic letter of
Acts 15:20–28 is presented as a directive sanctioned by
the Spirit. Paul's letters regularly issue what he deems

to be 'a command of the Lord' (1 Cor 14:37), and he sees his task as proclaiming not 'the word of men' but 'what it really is, the word of God' (1 Thess 2:13), both in his oral preaching *and* in his letters (2 Thess 2:15). His letters, then, are never merely private but always extend to a broader audience (2 Cor 1:1; 1 Thess 5:27; 1 Tim 3:14–15; Col 4:16; Philem 1–2). His self-awareness of writing divinely-binding Scripture is most pronounced when he instructs the Thessalonians essentially to excommunicate anyone who 'does not obey what we say in this letter' (2 Thess 3:14). Similar patterns appear in John 20:30–31, Hebrews 13:22, 1 John 2:7–8, and Jude 3.

In short, the evidence shows that the OT and NT authors shared a prophetic or apostolic consciousness that they were speaking from God. Peter captures this when he places his 'second letter' in the category of the 'predictions of the holy prophets' and the 'commandment of the Lord and Savior through your apostles' (2 Pet 3:1–2)—the OT and burgeoning NT, respectively.

'DEPOSIT OF WRITINGS'

It has become popular in some circles to assert that God's Word is not really found in *written* Scriptures but in a *person* (Jesus), with the Scriptures as merely a conduit to experience him. While this idea's heart may be in the right place—and while it is certainly true that Jesus Christ is the enfleshed 'Word' (John 1:1–2, 14)—this negativity towards the written-ness of Scripture is out of step with the evidence. From the earliest indications in the Torah (Exod 17:4) to the final chapter (Rev 22:18–19), God underscores his choice to reveal himself through inscripturated *writings*. Christians (and Jews) are profoundly people of the book.

The fact that the permanent form of their inspired communication is *written* (not oral, pictorial, dramatic, or any other medium) is emphasized for nearly every OT author: e.g., Moses (Exod 24:4); Joshua (Josh 24:26); Samuel (1 Sam 10:25); Solomon (Prov 22:30); Isaiah (2 Chr 26:22); Jeremiah (Jer 36:4); Daniel (Dan 7:1). The charter document of Israel is repeatedly called the '*Book* of the Covenant' (Exod 24:7), which is broadened to '*Book* of Moses' in reference to the whole Torah (Ezra 6:18). Daniel refers to prophecies he found in 'the books' (Dan 9:2). Even as early as the second century BC, the Jewish Scriptures were known as '*the* book' (*Letter of Aristeas* 316; Bar 4:1; Sir 24:23). Such an emphasis carries over into the Christian era. NT authors regularly introduce OT quotations with 'as it is *written*.' Jesus speaks of the '*Book* of Moses' (Mark 12:26), which Paul collapses further to 'when Moses is *read*' (2 Cor 3:15). Jesus speaks of a '*Book* of the Psalms' (Luke 20:42) and the '*reader*' of Daniel (Mark 13:14).

Emphasis on the written nature of NT documents is even more self-evident: Luke's prologues (Luke 1:3; Acts 1:1), Paul's epistolary greetings, John's reference to '*books* that could be *written*' (John 21:25), and emphasis on the authors' *written* instructions (Heb 13:22; 1 Pet 5:12; 1 John 1:4; Jude 3).

We can even say that all of God's covenantal dealings

(more below) are conceptualized as *written*. First in external form, on tablets and in a book (Exodus 19–24), then in internal form: 'I will put my laws in their minds and *write* them on their hearts' (Heb 8:10, citing Jer 31:33). To this 'writings' emphasis I add the modifier 'deposit,' drawing on the imagery of 2 Timothy 1:14. Scripture is a coherent collection—a permanent deposit of God's self-disclosure, which if left merely oral would have faded to gray—to be guarded and used to shape the people of God (2 Tim 3:16b).

'RECEIVED AS DIVINELY AUTHORITATIVE'

Canon scholars commonly speak about how rabbis or church councils conferred authority on a given writing, declaring it to be canonical and, thus, binding. That is, someone 'picked' the books and invested them with decisive authority. This view assumes authority is something *we* bestow. In some areas of life this is true: we collectively decide (through our elected representatives) the speed limit on a stretch of highway, for instance.

But if the 'inspired' element of our definition is correct, then the authority of the deposit of writings is not something we confer, but it is inherent in *what they are*. It is a divine authority by virtue of the author (God)—not the recipient (us). *By definition* Scripture contains within it the irreducibly ultimate authority or jurisdiction over all matters of doctrine and practice. We could no more possess the right to confer authority on *divine* writings than we could pick our birth parents and give them authority over us. They have it simply by virtue of what they are. This may sound circular ('Scripture is divinely authoritative because it is Scripture')—because it *is*. But such is true for all ultimate authorities. No one picked Planck's Constant or Avogadro's Number or Pi. They just simply *are*. The same is true for Scripture, if it is what it says it is.

What are some other examples of ultimate authorities?

This concept is precisely what we find in early Christian sources. They refer to the NT as writings that were 'handed down' (Clement of Alexandria, *Strom.* 3.13.93; *Ep. Diognetus* 11.1), 'received' (Gelasian Decree), and 'delivered unto our fathers...and confirmed as divine' (Athanasius). There is no talk of 'picking.' The inspired writings were handed down as from God and simply received/acknowledged as divinely authoritative.

'FOR THE COVENANT COMMUNITY'

The final element of the proposed definition is obvious from the names of the two halves of the modern Bible, but it often goes overlooked. Numerous communications were 'inspired' by God but never permanently recorded (e.g., much of Elijah's preaching). Numerous 'writings' also circulated within ancient Israel and the apostolic church (more on this below) but were never acknowledged as divinely authoritative. Hence one final piece is necessary: Scripture is only *that which God intended to be documentation of his covenant.*

Over the past century, in part stimulated by extensive study of ancient Near Eastern covenants, there has been a revival of the notion that the OT and NT are inherently covenants in *content* and *form*. There is no doubt that the *content* of God's relationship with his people is covenantal; the word shows up nearly 300x! This is essential in Jewish tradition. And while Christian groups nuance things differently, there is general agreement that God is in covenant with his people, unfolding from Adam (Gen 3) and Noah (Gen 6–9), to Abraham and the patriarchs (Gen 12–22), to Moses (Exod 19–34) and David (2 Sam 7), to the post-exilic community (Isa 42:6; Jer 31:30–33; Ezek 16:59), and to Jesus Christ (Luke 22:20).

But it is also clear from recent studies that the *form* of Scripture is intrinsically covenantal as well. Ancient covenants articulate the *historical basis* of a relationship between two parties, outline the *obligations* on each party, hold out *blessings for obedience* (and warnings for disobedience), establish *signs for enacting the covenant* (often the shedding of blood), and mandate permanent *written documentation.*

This is precisely what we see for the OT. The Torah in particular is called 'covenant law' (Exod 31:18; Ps 50:16), containing all the elements outlined above and concluding with a mandate to 'write very clearly' the covenant when Israel enters the promised land (Deut 27:1–8). But this covenantal shape encompasses the whole OT: the historical writings describe the basis of the relationship between God and his people; the legal codes establish the obligations, blessings, and warnings that flow from God's redemption of his people (Exod 19:4–5; 20:1); the wisdom and poetic writings describe what life looks like in covenant with God; and the prophetic writings proclaim and apply the covenant promises and stipulations. For good reason it is called a 'testament,' a term derived from the Latin for 'covenant.'

After Jesus' resurrection, his authorized witnesses recognize—based on his own words (Matt 26:28; Luke 22:20)—that they have entered into a new stage in God's covenant relationship (Heb 8–9). Not only do they regularly default to connecting written 'Scripture' with God's covenant promises (Gal 3:8), but as Jews who inherited the idea that covenant-entails-documentation, they would have assumed a 'new covenant' would likewise involve new writings. This gave the NT authors a grid for understanding what exactly they were producing. The Gospels and Acts are the new historical writings that root themselves explicitly in the fulfillment of the old covenant (e.g., Matt 1:1) and see the work of Jesus as the historical basis of a renewed relationship with God. The epistles shape the community with covenantal obligations, blessings, and warnings that flow from the work of Christ. The wisdom writings (primarily James, but elements of others) describe life in the new covenant. And the prophetic writings (Revelation; Olivet Discourse, Matt 24–25) proclaim and apply the covenant—even *concluding* the new covenant Scriptures with a reiteration of the essential covenant promise (Rev 21:3).

I call it a 'revival' because this appreciation of the covenantal nature of Scripture has deep roots. Among early Jews it was common to refer to Scripture as the 'book of the covenant' (Sir 24:23; 1 Macc 1:56-67). Likewise early Christians refer to the OT and NT as 'both covenants' (Melito of Sardis, Irenaeus, and Tertullian) and the 'encovenanted books' (Origen, *Comm. John* 5.4; Eusebius, *Hist.* 3.9.5). Most impressively, Cyril of Jerusalem calls them 'God-inspired writings of the old and new covenant' (*Cat.* 4.33; note the singular 'covenant').

In sum, when we refer to the Scriptures as the 'Old Testament' and 'New Testament' in English, we are not merely labeling the two parts of the modern Bible. We are tapping into the very essence of what they are as *covenant* documents, and what they document— God's saving work within the covenant community. If Scripture is, therefore, the inspired writings received as divinely authoritative *and* intended by God to function as covenantal documents, then there is by definition a boundary as to *what is* and *what is not* included (see Deut 4:1–2; 31:24–26; John 20:30; Rev 22:18–19). Covenant documentation is not open-ended. The covenantal principle carries with it the expectation—indeed, the

The same is true for modern covenants. For instance, when purchasing a house, there is a boundary between what is part of the legal documentation and what is, say, just a bill of materials.

requirement—that there be a clear delimitation as to what is intended to be part of that documentation.

WHAT SHOULD WE BE LOOKING FOR IN TRACING THE ORIGINS OF THIS DEPOSIT?

I have tried to define the 'divine deposit' of Scripture as precisely as possible, for only then can we go about tracing its origins and development. When we turn to study 'canon' and 'text', what should we expect to observe?

As mentioned above, one school of thought is that the church simply imposed Scriptural status on books and established the accepted text. This view is common within Roman Catholicism (and to a lesser degree, Eastern Orthodoxy) and the scholarly guild. It is inherently problematic. Until the Council of Trent (1543–1563), which *did* attempt to impose a canon and a text (Latin Vulgate), there is no sense in church history that the church exercises the privilege of deciding on God's behalf what is and what is not his inspired Word. It is Scripture *as covenant documentation* that creates the covenant community of the church, not the other way around!

A second school of thought is that the 'canon' of Scripture emerged from a process of selection from among a group of contestants based on external criteria. This is a common Protestant view, and while it contains true elements, it stumbles at two points. (i) It assumes someone at some point said, 'We need to have a canon, so let us rally the troops and hash it out.' Based on extant sources, *this never happened*. The so-called Council of

Jamnia (late 1st century AD) where rabbis picked the Jewish canon has proven to be an myth. Nor did such a process happen at Nicaea (325 AD), where canon was not even discussed; Constantine did not pick anything; and even the church councils that did discuss canon simply set forth what was already in use.

(ii) This framework also assumes someone drew up a list of criteria by which the good could be filtered from the bad. For the OT this includes named authorship, composition in Hebrew, and date; for the NT this includes pre–100 AD date, apostolic authorship, orthodox content, and widespread usage. While these features are important, they are never *imposed as criteria*, and if they were, they would often fail! For instance, some Jewish writings are fairly ancient and originally written in Hebrew (Sirach, Tobit), and the date of some received as canonical is disputed (Daniel). On the NT side, some writings are possibly pre-100 AD (*1 Clement, Didache*), ascribed to apostolic men (*Barnabas*), basically orthodox (Polycarp's epistles), and widely used (*Shepherd of Hermas*), but none of these were ever considered by large parts of the church to be inspired Scripture. Moreover, if someone 'picked' the books, why would they have done it this way? Why Chronicles, with its overlaps with Samuel–Kings? Why *four* Gospels, when so many tensions are introduced? Ultimately, the notion of 'canonization' as a sifting process whereby a writing 'makes it into the canon' is fundamentally flawed.

Where does that leave us? *Scripture authenticates itself by virtue of what it is.* It is not waiting around for rabbis or bishops to grant it inspired, authoritative, covenantal status. A scriptural writing already possesses it from its point of composition by God to be covenantal deposit. In other words, a Scriptural writing—if it is truly that— is inherently canonical. It imposes itself. What is our job? Simply *to recognize or receive it as such.* God did not drop golden tablets from heaven. Rather, covenantal Scriptures were composed over time and copied by hand, and throughout the process people in the covenant community discern the voice of God through *these* books such that they receive them with gladness.

As with the rest of the covenant relationship, then, we should not expect to find this process of recognition and transmission to be neat and tidy. It took time for the covenant community to recognize the divine qualities of Scripture and submit to its authority and community-transforming power. If the covenant people of Israel nearly lost their Scriptures at one point (2 Kgs 22), we should not expect the process to be smooth! Not everyone agreed at every point along the way. But this does not negate the premise of a self-authenticating and bounded set of inspired Scriptures. It is simply what we would expect when divine providence is at work among sinful people.

SUMMARY

Taking stock, I have proposed that Scripture is *the inspired deposit of writings received as divinely authoritative for the covenant community.* When I use 'Scripture' throughout the rest of the book, I will be doing so in that sense. A few other clarifications are needed.

First, 'Scripture' needs to be distinguished from 'Bible.' The former develops over time. For instance, 'Scripture' in the time of Joshua included the first five books. 'Scripture' in the time of Paul included only the old covenant writings and, perhaps, some Gospels and James. 'Bible,' on the other hand, refers to the final product after all the writings are completed. Something can be 'scriptural' before the final scope of the 'Bible' is solidified. I will generally use 'Scripture' over 'Bible.'

Second, we also must distinguish 'Scripture' and 'canon.' Let me illustrate. The Beatles produced a certain number of songs (and only those). This authentic set of songs simply is what it is. But any music collector or record company could try to put together a collection of the full set, and they might disagree at points: accidentally exclude a song, add a single by Paul McCartney they confused as a Beatles song, or even throw out *Sgt. Pepper* altogether. But such Beatles 'canons' do not decide *what the actual authentic songs are*, but simply provide perspectives on what they might be. The fault for conflicting canons lies with us, not the Beatles.

If a group's list of canonical books disagrees with another, who is to blame? The one who made the books, or the list-maker?

In the same way, biblical 'canon' is not itself the authoritative rule imposed to define Scripture (though this misconception is extremely common). Indeed, the very idea and terminology of 'canon' did not even emerge until several centuries after the old and new covenant Scriptures were already recognized. Rather, 'canon' is better understood as the *output*—not the *input*—of the process of fallible Jews/Christians recognizing the shape and extent of the writings received as divinely authoritative Scriptures. Canon does not bestow authority but presumes it. No one 'opened' or 'closed' the canon; God did. Thus, I will use 'canon' to designate the end result of recognizing the shape or boundaries of those writings *received as Scripture* (as defined above). Various 'canons' may circulate, but that is more an issue with the receivers (us) than the sender (God).

Third, if 'Scripture' is defined this way, the *words* we care most about are the ones given by God in the original form of those writings. In God's providence, we do not have the actual artifacts (stone tablets, papyrus, etc.) containing the initial inscripturation of those words. Rather, the words were handed down orally and in written copies over a long period of time. This inextricably human process introduced erroneous wording in the manuscripts. That is simply what we would expect and presents no challenge whatsoever to the essence and authority of Scripture. They do, however, force us to work diligently to recover the *words* as given.

The table has been set. Let us proceed with the first main course: Old Testament canon (ch. 2) and text (ch.3).

2

OT CANON:

DO WE HAVE THE RIGHT BOOKS?

Ask anyone who has tried a 'read-through-the-Bible-in-a-year' plan, and they probably relived Israel's fate and lost steam somewhere in Numbers. For many, Israel's Scriptures are quite foreign—recording events, poetry, prophecies, and teachings of a time and place removed from us by millennia. Many Christians ignore them, due to theological reasons or the intimidation factor.

The complexity of the OT is worsened by how different combinations of books are accepted as canonical. Modern Jewish, Roman Catholic, Eastern Orthodox, and Protestant traditions fully agree on thirty-nine of the books (Genesis through Malachi). The Protestant tradition agrees with Judaism in stopping there. But the

RC & Orthodox Include: 1–2 Maccabees, Tobit, Judith, Additions to Esther, Wisdom of Solomon, Sirach, Baruch, Epistle of Jeremiah, Additions to Daniel

Orthodox Bible Additions: 1 Esdras, 3 Maccabees, Prayer of Manasseh, Psalm 151 (with 4 Maccabees and 2 Esdras included in an appendix)

Ethiopic church adopts the Orthodox collection but adds Jubilees, 1 Enoch, 4 Esdras, and Paralipomena Baruch

Roman Catholic and Orthodox Bibles include other books *as Scripture*.

What is going on? Why are there so many different Old Testaments running around? How did we get there, and what should we make of this? Is my personal copy the 'right' one? Are these other books dangerous?

This chapter aims to answer these important questions. As we will see, the origins of the books of the OT and the process of receiving it as Scripture are, indeed, quite complex. The data indicate that the Jewish/Protestant canon has the strongest argument in its favor, but I hope to assess things fairly. I will first discuss where the OT came from and how it took shape; I will then take us on a journey through how early Jews and, subsequently, early Christians received the OT scriptural deposit; finally I will address these 'other' books.

HOW DID THE OT DEPOSIT OF WRITINGS TAKE SHAPE IN ANCIENT ISRAEL?

Israel's Scriptures were composed during a one thousand-year period from ~1400 BC to ~400 BC—or ~1200 BC to ~200 BC for those who hold to later dating. Most books have identifiable authors, though some are formally anonymous. The majority was written in Hebrew, with ~1.2% in Aramaic (portions of Genesis, Ezra, Jeremiah, Daniel). The books were written during peace and crisis, mostly in Israel though some elsewhere.

This unparalleled book-of-books was set forth in writing as God worked out the covenant progressively in history: the era of the patriarchs (Genesis–Deuteronomy), pre-monarchy (Joshua–Ruth), monarchy (Samuel, Kings, most poetic/wisdom books), exilic period (most prophets, Esther), and post-exilic restoration (Ezra–Nehemiah, Haggai–Malachi, Chronicles). As redemption unfolded over time, God gave inspired writings to shape the covenant community over time as well.

Scripture, then, was a progressive deposit. We see fascinating signs of this in the OT, as earlier Scriptures were received as divinely authoritative downstream in the life of the covenant community. That is, later inspired writers acknowledged prior inspired writers. This 'inner-biblical' pattern can be traced across three categories of Scripture.

Torah

Immediately after it was set forth in writing, the Torah (Genesis–Deuteronomy) was cited in Joshua 8:31–32 and 23:6. The narrative of the Torah is referenced in 1 Samuel 12:8, and the 'Law of Moses' is acknowledged as divinely-given Scripture in the monarchic era (1 Kgs 2:3; 2 Kgs 14:6; 2 Chr 23:18). Psalm 119 repeatedly ascribes the 'law of Moses' as given directly by God.

Though the Torah suffered a lapse of usage in the years before Josiah (2 Kgs 22), in the exilic/post-exilic period it is cited authoritatively (Ezra 3:2; 9:9–12; Dan 9:11–13) and stimulated renewal (Neh 8:1–9:38). In fact, the role of the writing prophets can be understood as the preaching of Torah to the covenant people. Even the Persian king Artaxerxes recognized the Torah as the 'law of God' for Israel (Ezra 7:25–26). The first five books are the indisputable nucleus of the divine deposit.

Prophetic writings

The writers of the post-Torah historical books—Joshua, Judges, 1–2 Samuel, 1–2 Kings—are typically denoted 'former' prophets. They inscripturated the 'words the LORD of hosts sent by his Spirit' (Zech 7:12). Several portions of 'former prophets' are received and incorporated fully into later writings, such as the reuse of 2 Kings 18:13–20:11 in Isaiah 36:1–38:8 and 2 Kings 24:18–25:30 in Jeremiah 52. The author of Chronicles interacts greatly with the earlier Samuel and Kings. And 2 Chronicles 24:27 refers to a commentary written about 1–2 Kings that indicates it had been received as authoritative (and thus deserving a commentary!). It is evident that these 'former' prophetic writings were acknowledged very early in the life of Israel.

The same is true for the 'latter' prophets, such as Isaiah, Jeremiah, Ezekiel, and the twelve minor prophets. A 'written' form of 'the vision of Isaiah' is referenced in 2 Chronicles 32:32. Jeremiah cites Micah 3:12 in 26:16–18. Ezra (1:1) and Daniel (9:2), in turn, cite the 'word of the LORD given to Jeremiah.' Ezra 5:1 appeals to the prophetic work of Haggai and Zechariah. In short, very early in the exilic and post-exilic periods, the writings of 'latter' prophets were acknowledged.

Other writings

Some OT writings are not referenced within the OT itself, which is understandable due to their later dates or limited scope. However, the proverbs are acknowledged in 1 Kings 4:32. Additionally, 2 Samuel 22 reuses Psalm 18. 1 Chronicles 16:8–36 features an impressive stitching together of three psalms (Ps 105:1–15; 96:1–13; 106:1, 47–48). Some argue that 2 Samuel 7 draws on Psalm 89, and there are numerous indications that the author of Job is interacting with the psalms.

Not every citation of a prior scriptural writing within another scriptural writing *guarantees* that it was received as divinely-inspired covenant documentation. However, the overall pattern—even if some data points could be debated—is that later inspired writers were acknowledging the divine authority, the Scriptural status, of antecedent writings remarkably early. They did not wait for a later council!

Signalling the sacred books

This becomes all the more apparent when one observes how these writers were well aware of other 'books,' 'records,' and 'annals.'

Yet they appear to draw a clear distinction between the Scriptural ones, to which they predicate 'word of the LORD,' and the others to which they do not. Those are simply sources of information. For that reason, it is unsurprising that none were retained

How did Israel indicate the difference between the Scriptural writings and the 'nice-to-have-but-not-Scriptural' ones? The tabernacle, and later the temple, apparently functioned as a sacred repository marking off Scriptures given by God.

From the beginning, the Israelites placed the 'Book of the Covenant' in the ark inside the temple/tabernacle (Exod 25:16; Deut 10:2). Later Samuel wrote the instructions for the kingship 'in a book and laid it up before the LORD' (1 Sam 10:25). Hilkiah reports how he discovered 'the book of the Law in the house of the LORD,' where it lay stored but unused (2 Kgs 22:8).

Later Jewish historians likewise speak of 'Scripture which is laid up in the temple' and the 'books laid up in the temple' (Josephus, *Ant.* 3.1.7 and 5.1.17, respectively). The *Letter of Aristeas* (line 176) describes how the high priest of the temple approved the copies of the Jewish

Evidence that writers of the OT were aware of other writings: Wars of the Lord (Num 21:14); Jashar (Josh 10:12–13); Acts of Solomon (1 Kgs 11:41); Chronicles of the Kings of Israel and Judah (1 Kgs 14:19, 29; 2 Chr 16:11); Samuel the Seer, Nathan the Prophet, and Gad the Seer (1 Chr 29:29); Prophet Nathan; Ahijah the Shilonite; Iddo (2 Chr 9:29); Prophet Shemaiah (2 Chr 12:15); Jehu son of Hanani (2 Chr 20:34); King David (1 Chr 27:24); Book of Annals (Neh 12:23); Kings of Media and Persia (Est 10:2)

Scriptures being sent to Egypt. And 1 Maccabees describes how the Greek soldiers who defiled the Jerusalem temple in 168 BC burned 'the books of the law that they found' (1:54–57). In short, the Israelites and post-exilic Jews signaled their regard for divinely-given Scriptural books by depositing them in the house of God.

Closure

Why did the writings cease? What 'closed' this collection of Scriptural books if it was not some sort of ecclesiastical committee meeting? Here the notion of Scripture as covenant documentation provides a solution. All the inspired OT writings were produced during the period of time in which God was manifestly present with his people, when the promises of the old covenant were still unfolding, and when his Spirit was giving divine words to the prophets. However flawed Israel was, it was nevertheless the golden age of the covenant. But as any reader of the OT knows, this came to crashing end.

The covenantal curse of exile was poured out on Israel (722 BC) and Judah (605–586 BC). As Ezekiel painfully depicts, the 'glory' of the Lord departed from the Jerusalem temple (11:22–25). And while there was a partial restoration of the covenant community after the exile (Neh 8–10), the OT concludes with a painful sense of unfinished business. The 'glory' never returns to the rebuilt temple (Mal 3:1), and after the failed reboot of the monarchy, the prophetic word ceases. Indeed Joel and Ezekiel speak of a day when the Spirit of prophecy will return (2:28–29; 36:26–27, respectively), and Malachi, the last inspired prophet, declares the 'law of Moses' must sustain the people until prophecy returns (4:4–5). God, in other words, closed the OT Scriptures—withdrew his Spirit from inspiring covenantal Scriptures—when the 'old covenant' was left unfulfilled and awaiting the new.

This cessation of Spirit-inspired prophecy after the 400s BC is attested in several early Jewish writings (1 Macc 4:46; Prayer of Azariah 15; Josephus, *Apion* 1.8; *2 Apoc Bar* 85.3) as well as the New Testament (Heb 1:1; Matt 11:13). By the early rabbinic period the consensus is that after 'the death of the last prophets, Haggai, Zechariah, and Malachi, the Holy Spirit departed from Israel' (*b. Sanh.* 11a and elsewhere).

Let us summarize. By the 400s BC, there was a clear 'inner-biblical' awareness of a collection of writings given by the Spirit of God, received as covenant Scripture for Israel, and deposited in the temple. The shape/boundaries of these Scriptures may not yet have reached full recognition, but that does not undermine how God had, by definition, 'closed the canon' through the cessation of divinely-inspired scriptural writings.

HOW WAS THE OT DEPOSIT RECEIVED WITHIN EARLY JUDAISM?

Stepping forward in time, how did Jews leading up to (and shortly after) the time of Christ view this OT deposit of Scripture? We will take it in three steps: confirmation of the threefold shape; reception of individual books; and indications that the writings were viewed as divinely-given Scripture.

Crystallizing the threefold shape

Everyone acknowledges that a basic education consists of 'Three Rs': reading, writing, and 'rithmetic. We may debate where to slot 'social studies.' But few deny that these three categories segment what proper education is. This analogy can help us understand the way the OT Scriptures were received.

Today the Hebrew Scriptures are segmented into three categories collectively labeled the 'Tanak': 'T' for Torah, 'N' for Nevi'im (Prophets), and 'K' for Ketuvim (Writings). These threefold divisions clarify the shape of the Scriptures recognized to be from God. But the segmentation is no late innovation. It emerges in Israel itself: Zechariah gives evidence (7:12), as do Jeremiah ('law...counsel from the wise...word from the prophet,' 18:18) and Ezekiel ('vision from the prophet...law... counsel from the elders,' 7:26). Its crystallization over time—without any outside 'decision' imposing it—gives insight into the Jewish community's canonical awareness.

The first post-biblical indication of a threefold division is found in the ~180 BC prologue to the Wisdom of Ben Sira (or Sirach): 'Many great teachings have been given to us through the *law* and the *prophets* and *the others that followed them.*' The third category—also called 'the rest of the books' twice more—is fuzzy at this stage, but clearly recognized.

This threefold division may be found in the ~1st CBC 'Sectarian Manifesto' of the Dead Sea Scrolls. Though fragmentary, it appears to reference 'the book of Moses, the book[s of the Pr]ophets, and Davi[d]' (4Q397 frag. 14–21). The 'and David' is cryptic but likely refers to a loose third category headed by the davidic Psalms. A similar use of 'David' is found in 2 Maccabees, which acknowledges the Torah and prophets (2:13; 15:9), and a 'library' containing 'books about the kings and prophets, and the writings of David, and letters of kings' (2:13–14). In the first century AD, Philo (*Cont.* 25) and Josephus (*Apion* 1.38–14) speak of Law/ Moses, prophets, and 'hymns/psalms.' Fourth Maccabees mentions the law, prophets, and (at least) proverbs as part of the 'Scriptures of Israel' (18:10–18). The threefold shape of the Scriptures received as canonical clearly goes back early in Judaism, reaching its formal designation as Torah, Prophets, and Writings in ~150–180 AD (an early tannaitic saying cited in *b. Batra* 14b).

Not everyone acknowledged the latter two categories. The Samaritans and, arguably, Sadducees only received the Torah. But even this rejection of the Prophets and Writings *implies* that they were categories that could be accepted/rejected in the first place.

Clarifying the books in each of the three divisions

The threefold shape was acknowledged early on. But what about the individual books? As we might expect, the providential process by which the Jewish community received individuals books as inspired, covenantal Scripture—especially the later ones whose ink was still wet, so to speak—took some time. There were debates in particular about the 'Writings' (especially Song of Songs, Proverbs, Esther, and Ecclesiastes), which is unsurprising as it is the fuzziest category. But overall we see substantial agreement on what makes up the threefold canon.

Josephus, for instance, writes: 'we do not have an innumerable multitude of books...but only twenty-two books'—five of Moses, thirteen Prophets, and four Writings (*Apion* 1.38–41). Another Jewish writer references 'twenty-four books' that are decisive for Jews (*4 Ezra* 14.44–45), and this numbering is later sanctioned in *b. Batra* 14b. The Christian writer Epiphanius cites his copy of the early Jewish writing *Jubilees* (~2nd century BC) as mentioning 'twenty-two books.' But the modern Christian OT has 39. So which is it?

The solution is reassuringly simple, as each numbering system refers *to the same set of books*, just arranged differently, via conforming the numbering to the 22-letter Hebrew or 24-letter Greek alphabet.

Also, there was a bit of fluidity in the sequencing of the books in the 'K'/Writings. Unlike the Torah or historical prophets, there was no inherent sequence to these writings, nor was there a way to be consistent in an era in which the Hebrew Scriptures were on separate scrolls. Only with the switch to the codex (book) technology could there be a linear way to order the books, but even early codices do not always agree.

24–book Tanak (used by Jews today)

Torah	5 (Gen.–Deut.)
'N'/Prophets	4 'former' (Josh., Judg., Sam., Kings)
	4 'latter' (Isa., Jer., Ezek., 'Minor')
'K'/Writings	3 books (Psalms, Prov., Job)
	5 scrolls/megilloth (Song, Ruth, Lam., Eccl., Esth.)
	3 others (Dan., Ezra-Neh., Chron.)

22–book Tanak (referenced by Josephus)

Torah	5 (Gen.–Deut.)
'N'/Prophets	(–1) Treat Sam.-Kings as one book
'K'/Writings	(–1) Bundle Lam. with Jer.

39–book OT (used by Christians today)

Torah	5 (Gen.–Deut.)
'N'/Prophets	(+11) Count Minor prophets individually
	(+2) Break Sam. and Kings into their halves
'K'/Writings	(+1) Break Chron. into its halves
	(+1) Count Ezra and Neh. individually

Signaling the writings received as divinely authoritative

The Jewish community indicated their recognition of these books *as Scripture* by a variety of signs. None of these is necessarily decisive, but the cumulative effect is clear. First, several writers speak explicitly about their high regard for these writings. The Jews in the Dead Sea area attest David wrote the Psalms under 'spirit of prophecy which had been given to him from the Most High' (11Q5). The *Letter of Aristeas* refers to the 'books' as 'divine law' (line 3). And per Josephus, 'all Jews, immediately, and from their very birth, esteem these books to contain divine doctrines' (*Apion* 1.8).

Second, it appears that most Jewish communities continued Israelite tradition by storing their Scriptural books, distinct from other writings, in a container called the *tevah/bimah* in the synagogue. Philo observes that the Scriptures were kept in a 'sacred shrine' in each worship-house of the Jewish sect of the Therapeutae (*Cont.* 25). More explicitly, in Luke 4:16–20 the synagogue attendant retrieves the Isaiah scroll for Jesus when he visits to preach.

Third, from the earliest days of Judaism, the Hebrew Scriptures were used in liturgy and worship: i.e. the use of the Hallel psalms (Pss 113–118), the reading of the Megilloth in the synagogue, and use of the psalms by the Jews at Qumran.

Fourth, the Jewish authors of non-scriptural writings cite the Hebrew Scriptures extensively. The list of quotations/allusions of the Tanak in intertestamental writings would be too long to provide here (see Tob 2:1 as an example). Now, we must reiterate that citing a book does not automatically indicate it was received as divinely-inspired Scripture. In the Dead Sea Scrolls, for instance, the *Apocryphon of Joshua* is quoted in 4Q175. But the books of the Tanak were cited substantially more often than others.

Fifth, we can point to how the Scriptures were handled and treated. The books received as Scripture were, on the whole, copied far more frequently than others (i.e. all OT books were found in multiple copies at Qumran except for Esther). They were also typically copied onto more durable material, feature certain scribal patterns like the reverential treatment of YHWH, and copied only on one side of the scroll (though none of these are hard-and-fast rules). Typically only the scriptural books were deemed worthy of commentaries. And the earliest translation efforts into Greek and Aramaic clearly privileged the books received as Scripture.

No doubt the libraries of Jewish groups included non-Scriptural writings seen to be helpful—we will return to this below. But the evidence overwhelmingly indicates early recognition of a threefold deposit of Scriptures given by God, extensive agreement on the 22/24/39 books comprising it (with some fuzziness at the margins), and the divine status of those books.

HOW WAS THE OT DEPOSIT RECEIVED WITHIN EARLY CHRISTIANITY?

Why did I spend so much time on early Jewish reception of canonical writings? The reason is simple: Jesus and the apostolic church fully accepted the Hebrew Scriptures familiar to them from their Jewish background. There is no explicit list of accepted OT books in the NT—there was apparently no need for one. Jesus and Paul in particular never make the boundaries of the Scriptures a point of debate, but assumed they were on the same page in order to debate with their Jewish opponents on *interpreting* said Scriptures.

Though some Christians today downplay the OT, it

is clear that Jesus and his early followers fully receive *old covenant documentation as divinely authoritative.* This is stamped on every NT page, but some passages stand out. Paul asserts the gospel was 'pre-promised' in the holy Scriptures through the prophets (Rom 1:2), namely, the 'oracles of God' (Rom 3:2) that foretold the death/resurrection of the Christ (1 Cor 15:3–4). Peter, likewise, sees the 'word of the gospel' as something declared in the old covenant (1 Pet 1:24–25), with the OT prophets foretelling the 'grace' and the 'sufferings of Christ' (1:10–11). They got this idea from Jesus, who declares his sufferings fulfilled the OT (Luke 24:44–46).

With those clarifications, we can follow the same three steps (above) in exploring early Christian reception of the OT.

Affirming the threefold shape

The Gospels of John (1:45) and Luke (24:25) explicitly mention the same Torah and 'N'/Prophets categories introduced above. But what about the 'K'/Writings? Both Jesus and Peter indicate that the psalms were not some cloud of scattered poems but had already been solidified into the 'book of Psalms' attributed to David (Luke 20:42; Acts 1:20).

Moreover, Jesus may be giving an indirect indication of a threefold canon when he speaks of 'the blood of Abel to the blood of Zechariah' (Luke 11:51). The first martyr mentioned is found in Genesis 4—the first book of the Torah. The last one mentioned may refer to the prophet whose death is recorded in 2 Chronicles 24:20–22—the last book of the 'K'/Writings according to some sequencing. Is Jesus subtly indicating the bookends of his pew Bible? Maybe. But some early Jewish collections put Chronicles first in the 'K'/Writings, not last; Uriah in Jeremiah 26:20–23 is likely the last martyred prophet chronologically; and Matthew 23:35 appears to label this Zechariah as someone else.

Stronger evidence is Jesus' listing of 'the Law of Moses, the Prophets, and the Psalms' as 'the Scriptures' (Luke 24:44–45). Though we cannot be absolutely sure that Jesus is using 'Psalms' as a shorthand for all the 'K'/Writings received as Scripture at that point, his acknowledgement of Daniel (Mark 13:14) at least makes it possible. At a minimum, Jesus acknowledges the old covenant Scriptures to have a threefold shape.

Similar references can be found in post-apostolic writings. Clement of Rome describes 'the sacred books enjoined upon [Moses]…and the rest of the prophets followed' (*1 Clem* 43.1); he elsewhere cites from the 'K'/Writings. Melito of Sardis refers to the 'law and the prophets' (Eusebius, *Hist.* 4.26.13–14), though he later acknowledges several 'K'/Writings as Scripture. And Jerome refers to the OT as comprised of Moses, the Prophets, and the 'Hagiographa' (*Prologue to Samuel and Kings*). In short, the evidence cumulatively indicates that Jesus, the apostles, and the early church quite clearly acknowledged a three-part OT collection of writings.

Clarifying the books in each of the three divisions

The NT never opines directly on the list of received OT books. Some early Christians endorsed the 24-book listing (Jerome) while others followed 22 (Origen).

Perhaps the best way to get a handle on the specific OT books received by the early church among the threefold Scriptures is to examine their early attempts to list them. To keep things simple, I will tabulate these 'canon lists' by indicating Y when there is agreement with the received Jewish collection (provided above), or +/ – for any deviations:

	Torah	'N'/Prophets	'K'/Writings
Epiphanius (De mens. 22–23)	Y	Y	Y
Bryennios List (Jerusalem Codex)	Y	Y	Y
Origen (Eusebius, Hist. 6.25.2)	Y	+ Ep. Jeremiah	Y
Melito of Sardis (Eusebius, Hist. 4.26.14)	Y	Y	+ Wis. Sol. – Esther
Mommsen List (~359 AD)	Y	+ 1–2 Maccabees	+ Tobit + Judith + Ps 151 – Lamentations
Hilary of Poitiers (Prol. in Ps. 15)	Y	+ Ep. Jeremiah	+ Tobit + Judith
Athanasius (Festal Letter 39.4)	Y	+ Ep. Jeremiah + Baruch	– Esther
Council of Laodicea (Canon 60)	Y	+ Ep. Jeremiah + Baruch	Y
Cyril of Jerusalem (Catech. 4.35)	Y	+ Ep. Jeremiah + Baruch	Y
Gregory Nazianzus (Carm. 1.12.5)	Y	Y	– Esther
Jerome (Ep. 53.8)	Y	Y	Y

There is extensive agreement, but at the margins certain writings not received by the Jews were deemed scriptural by some Christians.

Signaling the writings received as divinely authoritative

Like their Jewish predecessors, early Christians did several things to indicate that they received the OT Scriptures as God-given. Their explicit affirmations of divine inspiration were outlined already in Chapter 1 (e.g., 2 Pet 1:21), and the apostles were preaching from the OT in corporate worship from the earliest days (Acts 2).

NT citations and allusions to the OT writings abound, though the situation is more complex than often acknowledged. On the one hand, we find clear use of nearly every book, with Esther, Song, Ecclesiastes, Ruth, and Lamentations receiving the least attention (or none at all). On the other hand, the NT authors cite or show indirect use of writings not received in the Jewish canon, including Wisdom of Solomon, 1 Maccabees, Sirach, *1 Enoch*, and *Assumption of Moses*. But citation≠canonical: these latter kinds of citations may say nothing about canonical reception, just as the former citations (or lack thereof) may not either. That said, doubtless the OT Scriptures influence the NT writers orders of magnitude greater than any other writings, which shows the clear trajectory of divine authority.

Finally, Christian manuscripts treated OT writings with high regard, reflected not only in the extensive numbers of individual copies preserved (particularly in

Greek) but also in such details as the way the divine name was handled, which they inherited from the Jews. OT quotations in NT manuscripts also typically received special scribal markings.

In sum, the early Christians from Jesus and the apostles onward appear united around a threefold deposit of writings recognized to be divinely authoritative over the new covenant community. They inherited this bookishness from their Jewish forefathers. But, as the evidence surveyed above indicates, there were debates at the margins whereby some early Christians deviated from the books of Scripture passed down from the Jews.

WHAT ABOUT ALL THESE OTHER BOOKS?

If you set foot in a church library, you will find hundreds of various Christian books (theology, fiction, biographies, study guides) alongside a few dozen copies of the Bible. And if you picked a 'Study Bible' in that library, you would find notes and perhaps full articles or confessions scattered throughout. If you were naïve about this situation, you might think that those 'other' writings, especially those inside the cover of the Bibles, were just as authoritative if not more so (due to quantitative disparity) than the Bible. This would, of course, be mistaken. Keep this in mind as we tackle the 'other' books.

As mentioned previously, contemporary Christian groups share a core of OT books but disagree on 'others' added to them. And as shown above, this complexity goes back quite early. What should we make of this situation?

Though the cessation of Spirit-inspiration in the post-exilic period brought an end to *scriptural* writings, the Jews did not stop literary activity altogether. Quite the contrary: the treasure of writings that emerged in the post-400s BC period far exceeds the quantity of writing in the Hebrew Scriptures! We will cover three categories: the apocrypha, pseudepigrapha, and desert discoveries.

Apocrypha

These are the most well-known and intriguing due to long-standing debates about whether they are to be received as divinely authoritative...or not. They were composed in the 300s BC–100s AD timeframe and were passed on in Greek, though some were composed in Hebrew/Aramaic and later translated.

How did some of these end up not only in early Christian 'canon lists' (see above) but also in the Roman Catholic and Eastern Orthodox Bibles?

Early evidence among Jews is mixed. The discovery of Hebrew/Aramaic versions of Tobit, Sirach, and Epistle of Jeremiah among the Dead Sea Scrolls shows that *some* non-Greek Jews were reading them. Judith and 1

Books of the Apocrypha

1 Maccabees	Sirach	Additions to Daniel (Susanna, Song of the Three Young Men, Prayer of Azariah, Bel & the Dragon)
2 Maccabees	Wisdom of Solomon	
1 Esdras	Baruch	
Tobit	Epistle of Jeremiah	
Judith	Psalm 151	[3 Maccabees]
Additions to Esther	Prayer of Manasseh	[4 Maccabees]

Maccabees were highly regarded due to their association with Hanukkah. But Sirach was the only apocryphal book taken seriously as a 'contender'—but the author, as the prologue above shows, distinguishes *even his own writing* from the threefold Scriptures.

There is little evidence that any substantial group of early Jews treated the apocryphal books *as Scripture*. Philo, though a consummate Greek-speaking Jew, pays them little attention; Josephus, also a Greek-influenced Jew, uses 1 Maccabees and 1 Esdras for historical data but excludes them from the '22-book' Scriptures. The Jewish translators Aquila and Symmachus ignored the apocrypha altogether. By the early rabbis, the distinction reflected in *4 Ezra* between the twenty-four books of Scripture and the 'seventy' that are merely useful had won the day, and 'Ben Sira and all books written from that point on' were ultimately rejected (*t. Yad.* 2.13).

The early Christian era is a bit murkier. As shown already, some early 'canon lists' include select apocryphal writings. Moreover, some famous Christian codices include various combinations of apocrypha alongside the Greek translations of the Hebrew Scriptures, though they do not agree on which extra books are included or in what sequence. Early quotations of apocrypha are quite frequent as well.

The apocrypha question comes to a head with Origen, Augustine, and Jerome. Origen, though acknowledging a 22-book Jewish canon, advocates receiving other books based on *church usage* (*Epist. ad Afr.* 4–5, 13). Augustine elaborates further. In his famous listing of the books

Some Early Quotations of the Apocrypha

Tobit—quoted by Polycarp

Judith—used by *1 Clement*

Sirach—quoted/paraphrased in *Didache* and *1 Clement*

Wisdom of Solomon—quoted in *Didache* and *1 Clement*; included in a list of NT books by Epiphanius and the Muratorian fragment (!)

Baruch—quoted by Irenaeus, Ambrose, Basil, Clement of Alexandria, Tertullian, and Theodoret, though they all believed it to be part of Jeremiah

Additions to Daniel—quoted by Irenaeus

Prayer of Manasseh—included in the *Apostolic Constitutions*

wherein the 'authority of the Old Testament is contained,' he includes most of the apocrypha, reasoning, 'They are to be reckoned among the prophetical books, since they have attained recognition as being authoritative' (*Doc. Chr.* 2.8). Further, in *City of God* he argues that the church should receive all the books contained in the Greek OT translation—including most of the apocrypha not received by the Jews—because 'the same Spirit of God' speaks in them (17.20; 18.36).

Jerome, however, holds a decisively different view. Admittedly, Jerome appears inconsistent at first blush, denying the apocrypha are scriptural in some places, but citing them in other places without distinction. He clarifies this pattern elsewhere: 'as, then, the church reads Judith, Tobit, and the books of the Maccabees, *but does not admit them among the canonical Scriptures*, so let it also read these two volumes for the edification of the people, not to give authority to doctrines of the church' (from his *Prologue to Wisdom and Sirach*; emphasis mine). Jerome's key distinction is that some books are worthy to be read as edifying, but they do not possess divine authority over doctrine. In his Vulgate translation of the Hebrew Scriptures, he tacks on the apocrypha at the end. In the preface, he explains why: 'the church indeed reads [them]...but does not receive them among the canonical books...[and] not for establishing the authority of ecclesiastical dogmas.'

Later Christian writers and councils tended to follow Augustine or Jerome. The broader collection received by Augustine won the day among the Eastern Orthodox church. However, it was Jerome who influenced the Reformers *and* the Roman Catholic Church during the time of the Reformation/Counter-Reformation.

In that era *Sola Scriptura* brought the issue to a head, for medieval Roman Catholicism appealed to the apocrypha to establish doctrines (works of mercy, mass for the dead, purgatory). The Reformed response developed over time. Wycliffe followed the distinction introduced by Jerome, as did Andreas Karlstadt and Luther—sandwiching the apocrypha between the OT and NT. Calvin rejected them outright (though he was well-read in them), while the Synod of Dort and Westminster Assembly further nuanced Jerome's distinction. The KJV relegated the apocrypha to appendix status. Later Protestant Bibles removed them altogether.

Meanwhile, things were shaking out in a rather

Why do you think later Protestant Bibles removed the apocrypha altogether? What would including them in an appendix signal to readers?

interesting fashion on the Roman Catholic side. Nicolas de Lyra wrote commentaries on the apocrypha but followed Jerome in declaring, 'Books which are not of the canon are received by the Church to be read for instruction in morals, but their authority is reckoned less fit for proving matters which come into dispute' (*Comm. Tobit*). Cajetus likewise designated the apocrypha 'not canonical' for doctrine but a lesser kind of 'canonical' for edification (*Comm. Esther*). In the famous Complutensian Polyglot, Cardinal Ximenes printed only the Hebrew Bible and deemed the apocryphal books 'outside the canon, which the church receives rather for edification of the people than to confirm authority of ecclesiastical dogmas.' Indeed, the major Roman Catholic scholars of the day *agreed with the Protestants* on the secondary status of the apocrypha— until the Council of Trent (1546) reversed course, largely in response to the Reformation itself:

> If any one receive not, as sacred and canonical, the said books entire with all their parts, as they have been used to be read in the Catholic Church, and as they are contained in the old Latin vulgate edition; and knowingly and deliberately condemn the traditions aforesaid; let him be anathema.

The 'said books' include those apocrypha listed earlier in this chapter. This decree ended the debate—mandating Jerome's Vulgate, yet ignoring his view of the contents! Though the Vulgate is no longer the only allowable text in Catholicism, the flattening of distinctions is still upheld: the apocrypha are deemed 'Deuterocanonical' (second-canon) and *equally authoritative* alongside the 'Protocanonical' Hebrew Bible.

Among Protestants today, the Church of England is mildly inconsistent on the apocrypha. Article 6 of the Articles of Religion in the *Book of Common Prayer* cites Jerome in affording them second-tier status. Yet the *First Book of Homilies*, commended by Article 35, cites various apocryphal writings indistinguishably from the OT or NT. Moreover, apocryphal excerpts occasionally show up in the Sunday lectionary. Elsewhere, no Protestant denominations make any real use of the apocrypha (even for 'edification'), and most congregants are largely unaware of them.

Pseudepigrapha

These writings, whose label means 'falsely attributed,' arose from the same context as the apocrypha, but few received serious consideration by Jews or early Christians. In fact, many barely survived if not for historical happenstance. They were composed and/or translated in numerous languages (Hebrew, Aramaic, Syriac, Greek, Slavonic, Ethiopic, Latin) in the 200s BC to 200s AD timeframe.

One could understand these writings as a kind of Jewish 'fan fiction' that elaborates on biblical stories/themes, particularly gravitating towards key figures like Adam, Enoch, Noah, Melchizedek, Jacob, and Elijah.

Only *1 Enoch* received sustained attention. Copies

Examples of the Five Categories in the Pseudepigrapha

Apocalypses (heavenly visions): 1 Enoch, 2 Enoch, 2 Baruch, 4 Ezra, Greek Apocalypse of Ezra

Testaments (exhortations to descendants): T. Twelve Patriarchs, T. Moses, T. Abraham, T. Job

Rewritten Bible (expansions on OT texts): Jubilees, Genesis Apocryphon, Pseudo-Philo

Legends (stories about biblical characters): Joseph and Aseneth, Life of Adam and Eve, Ascension of Isaiah, Exagoge of Ezekiel

Wisdom and Poetry (proverbs, hymns, etc.): Sibylline Oracles, Psalms of Solomon, Prayer of Joseph

were found among the Dead Sea Scrolls, and some early Christians—due to the fact that it is quoted in Jude 14–15—showed high regard for it (e.g., *Barnabas*, Justin Martyr, Tatian, Irenaeus, Tertullian, Origen). Other pseudepigrapha occasionally receive attention, such as *Jubilees* at Qumran, *4 Ezra* in *Barnabas*, and *Ascension of Isaiah* in Justin Martyr (and possibly Hebrews). But on the whole, these writings were seen as additional writings from Jewish communities about biblical things, but neither given nor received with any kind of divine authority.

Desert discoveries

These writings were composed in the 200s BC to 100s AD timeframe, mostly in Hebrew/Aramaic, and discovered in various parts of Palestine and Egypt. The most famous collection is the Dead Sea Scrolls, which were discovered at Qumran in 1947–1956. Of the 900+ fragmentary writings discovered among 11 caves, about 40% are biblical scrolls (more on this below), 30% are apocrypha/pseudepigrapha (i.e. *Jubilees*, Tobit, and Sirach), and 30% are writings specific to that community (i.e. *Damascus Covenant, Community Rule, War Scroll, Temple Scroll*).

So where does this leave us? What should we make of these 'other' writings showing up on some early Jewish and Christian bookshelves? On the one hand, they are very important writings that contribute to a fuller picture of the religious ideas and social/cultural practices among Jews (and the Greco-Roman world) leading up to the time of Jesus. Indeed, they are some of the *only* sources for that period. NT writers and early Christians show familiarity with these writings. Even for Protestants, the fact that over half of the worldwide church acknowledges some of these writings as deuterocanonical means that we should, at a minimum, be familiar with them.

On the other hand, the evidence suggests that clear lines of distinction must be maintained in terms of *what these writings are* and, thus, what kind of authority (if any) they possess. Here we will focus on the apocrypha: do they belong in the modern Bible? Our definition from Chapter 1 helps here. Recall that Scripture is a divine deposit: immediately inspired by the Spirit of God, inherently possessing divine authority, and given by God to be covenant documentation. Each of these is critically important, and in my judgment the apocrypha—though fascinating and helpful—fail on all three. First, if the OT, NT, and Jewish tradition are correct that the Holy

Spirit ceased inspiring prophetic writings after Malachi, then the later apocrypha cannot themselves be divinely inspired in the same way as the Hebrew Scriptures. Second, in contrast to the inner-biblical way whereby Hebrew Scriptures receive one another—progressively over time—as divinely authoritative, the apocrypha bear no such marks. Third, the Jewish community after Malachi was in an open-ended situation of exile, a position of covenant curse still awaiting the fulfillment of God's promises.

[handwritten margin note: DOESN'T MEET 3 CRITERIA OF SCRIPTURE]

Hence, in terms of the source of divinely-given authority over today's covenant community, I would side with the Jews, Jerome, the Reformers, and most pre-Trent Catholics: the Hebrew Scriptures are *the Scriptures* in the full sense—the apocrypha are something less.

Some apocryphal writings like Baruch (2:35) express hope for a covenant renewal in the future but do not see themselves as covenant writings. Indeed, Ben Sira sees the Hebrew Bible as 'the book of the covenant' (24:23)—but not is own writing.

SUMMARY

We have covered a lot of ground in this chapter. It is easily the longest and most complex in this book, so be encouraged! We have traced how the Hebrew Scriptures originated in the life of Israel, how they were recognized by Jews and Christians, and how we can wisely approach the 'other' writings that are accepted by some but not by others. The Roman Catholic and Orthodox (and to a lesser degree, Anglican) use of the apocrypha has better pedigree than often admitted. But I have argued that there are stronger reasons to recognize only the threefold collection—Torah, 'N'/Prophets, and 'K'/Writings—as *the divine deposit of Scripture*. We need not view other Jewish writings with fear or suspicion. But only with regards the 22/24/39-book Hebrew Scriptures can we say, with confidence, 'Thus says the LORD.'

OT TEXT:

DO WE HAVE THE RIGHT WORDS?

It seems like every year the misinformation-mill cranks back up to enlighten the minds of poor, misguided Christians to 'the truth' they never knew about the Bible. This shows up not only in canon debates but also in questions about whether we can trust the *text* of the biblical books. Consider Kurt Eichenwald in *Newsweek* in early 2015 ('The Bible: So Misunderstood It's a Sin'):

> No television preacher has ever read the Bible. Neither has any evangelical politician. Neither has the pope. Neither have I. And neither have you. At best, we've all read a bad translation—a translation of translations of translations of hand-copied copies of copies of copies of copies, and on and on, hundreds of times.

The claim is that your modern Bible is so far removed from the original that you cannot even say you have 'the Bible' at all.

No doubt this is a huge issue. Given that the original artifacts such as the stone tablets of the Ten Commandments or the original scrolls recorded by Isaiah have not survived the sands of time, do we have the 'right' *words* of the Bible? Can we have confidence that we know what was originally *written* in those books? Has God's Word been preserved in all ages, as the church has always affirmed, or has it been lost?

We will sort this out for the OT in this chapter: where our translations come from, how their sources were passed on to us, and what degree of confidence we have about accessing the original *words* of Scripture. We will cover the NT in Chapter 5.

WHERE DOES OUR ENGLISH BIBLE COME FROM?

Every modern Bible, whether physical or digital, comes from somewhere. And unless you know classical Hebrew (and Aramaic), the form in which you are accessing the words of OT Scripture is a translation of some kind. But where do these translations come from? The *Newsweek*

The introductions to the ESV and NIV state that they are based on the 'Masoretic Text of the Hebrew Bible found in Biblia Hebraica Stuttgartensia' (BHS). The KJV/NKJV uses the Bomberg/Ben Chayyim text, which differs from BHS in fewer than a dozen places. Likewise, the modern Greek Orthodox translations of the OT are based directly on 4th–5th century Greek codices, not on intermediate translations.

article claims they are 'bad translations [of] translations of translations of translations.' As if the Bible got to you in some sort of garbled telephone game.

This could scarcely be further from the truth. All legitimate modern Protestant and Catholic (excluding their deuterocanon) editions are translated *directly from the Hebrew Scriptures*, not from other translations. Yes, English translations are often indebted to the lyrical quality and turns-of-phrase of the historic King James Version. But they all go back to the Hebrew, which is acknowledged to be *the* form of the divine deposit. Some English translations may be 'good' or 'bad,' but that is more an issue with translation strategy (and human error) than with the source itself.

The real question is: do we have accurate copies of the Hebrew to translate from? Even casual readers bump into the following kinds of footnotes in the English Bible:

> Gen 4:8—Hebrew; Samaritan, Septuagint, Syriac, Vulgate add *Let us go out to the field*
> Gen 31:47—Aramaic *the heap of witness*
> Gen 37:3—See Septuagint, Vulgate; or (with Syriac) *a robe with long sleeves.* The meaning of the Hebrew is uncertain (ESV)

What on earth are those things? What is a 'Septuagint' or a 'Syriac'? Should I be concerned?

Not quite. Any translator of Hebrew writings that are over 2,500 years old admits the ancient manuscripts are not always perfect. They may have gaps or errors in spelling, word order, and so forth introduced by scribes who labored in a difficult, pre-computer workplace. We also may not always fully understand the vocabulary or grammar at certain points (consider how easy is it even in your native language to misunderstand a written message when the sender is not available to clarify).

In such cases, we do two things. We examine the best copies of the Hebrew available, which give us *primary access to the words of the divine deposit* of Scripture. We also look at ancient (not modern) translations of the Hebrew, which play a role as *witness to the deposit*.

HOW DO WE ACCESS
THE SCRIPTURAL DEPOSIT IN HEBREW?

The Hebrew (with bits of Aramaic) text of Israel's Scriptures has traveled to us today from the original authors along a lengthy, winding road of hand-copying, with two major stops along the way. Let us work our way forward in time to unpack this further.

Original composition

We do not have the 'autographs' prepared by the Israelite

Four Steps in the Process of Transmitting the OT:

1. Original Hebrew Scriptures (1,400-400BC)
2. Findings of the Judean Desert (200BC-100AD)
3. Masoretic Codices (900-1100AD)
4. Today (KJV, ESV, NIV, etc.)

authors—thankfully so, for no doubt we would invent all sorts of ways to idolize them. But we do know a few things about this early period. The earliest were originally written in a Phoenician or Paleo-Hebrew alphabet on scrolls using only consonants, with the vowels being passed down orally. In the late second millennium BC, there appears to have been an update to Hebrew grammar that led to minor updating of syntax (but not the content—Deut 4:2) of the early writings. Around the ninth century BC, some consonants started being used to indicate vowels (*matres lectionis*). And in the sixth century BC the Paleo-Hebrew letters were replaced with Aramaic or 'square' script (the 'yod' mentioned in Matthew 5:18 shows this was the form familiar to Jesus).

Unfortunately, while we have various inscriptions, coins, and other Israelite artifacts from this period, we do not have any copies of the Hebrew Scriptures (let alone the autographs). Thus, our primary access to the words of the scriptural deposit comes via two stages of later copies.

Findings of the Judean desert

The first period from which copies have survived is 200s BC to 100s AD. The oldest substantial collection of Hebrew Scriptures available are those from the Judean desert. The most famous were found in the caves of Qumran (east of Jerusalem), commonly known as the Dead Sea Scrolls (introduced above). They include fragments of all OT books except Esther (the most magnificent being the 'Great Isaiah Scroll'); *peshers* that feature a portion of biblical text along with commentary (especially an important one of Habakkuk); various scrolls containing copies of biblical psalms alongside other poetry; and quotations of the OT passages embedded in other writings.

Other Hebrew findings from the Dead Sea region are significant as well. The excavation of Wadi Murabba'at yielded fragmentary copies of Genesis, Deuteronomy, Isaiah, and the Minor Prophets. Among the remains of the synagogue at En Gedi is a charred lump of Leviticus; in 2016 an Israeli team successfully used 3-D micro-CT imaging to reconstruct the scroll and access its wording, revealing a close match to the known text. Further south, partial copies of Numbers, Deuteronomy, and the Psalms were discovered at Nahal Hever (along with twenty-four skeletons in the so-called 'Cave of Horrors'). Finally, in the synagogue of Masada were found fragments of Genesis, Leviticus, Deuteronomy, Psalms, and Ezekiel.

To these findings we may add the Nash Papyrus (~150 BC). This single page includes the 'Shema' (Deut 6:4) as well as an interesting composite rendering of the Ten Commandments from Exodus 20 and Deuteronomy 5. It was the oldest known Hebrew artifact until the discovery of the Dead Sea Scrolls.

Pausing to take inventory, this seminal stage provides priceless manuscript remains that give us the earliest access *in Hebrew* to the words of the original Scriptures. But nearly all of it is fragmentary. We could not stitch together a complete OT from these Judean remains, though some books would fare better than others.

Between this milestone and the next, the number of Hebrew artifacts is limited to a few partial copies from the third to seventh centuries.

Just because the remains of the Judean Desert are fragmentary does not mean they did not have complete copies in their day. They simply have decayed over time. It is amazing they survived at all.

Masoretes

The second major stop in the journey is the Masoretic period (500s–1000s AD). The Masoretes were an assorted group of rabbis who worked primarily in Babylon, Jerusalem, and Tiberia. They inherited the consonantal text of the Hebrew Scriptures—recall that the earliest forms lacked explicit vowels—and, as diligent textual scholars, made three major contributions:

- *Introducing a formal system of vowels* to conserve the pronunciation that had been passed down orally for centuries
- *Instituting a system of 'masora'* to annotate the sacred consonantal text (e.g., textual markings for spelling differences or suspected scribal errors; accent markings for liturgical use; counts of lines and words in a given book)
- *Stabilizing the wording* to reflect what they believed to be the most authentic (in two slightly different final forms, by Ben Asher and Ben Naphtali)

The climax of the work of the Masoretes is found in a handful of medieval manuscripts. The oldest is Codex Cairensis (~896 AD), containing only the prophets. The most accurate is the Aleppo Codex (~925 AD), but large portions are burned. The most important is arguably the Leningrad Codex (~1008 AD), which contains the earliest complete text and masora. It serves as the basis of the *Biblia Hebraica Stuttgartensia* (BHS) behind nearly all modern translations. Another manuscript containing the 'former' prophets was confirmed in 2017 to be from the same scribe as that of Leningrad.

There are other important Masoretic manuscripts from the 900s–1000s, though not quite as high-quality: the Eretz Israel Pentateuch; Damascus Pentateuch; London Codex; Sassoon 1053; Petersburg Codex; Vatican Urb. ebr. 2; and the Erfurt Codices. After this period, there is an explosion of Hebrew manuscripts that are very uniform, including those found in the Cairo Genizah (synagogue storeroom). Jewish medieval work on the Hebrew Scriptures culminated in the first printed edition in Italy in 1488. From this late medieval period, it is a straight shot from Hebrew to any modern language translation.

Connecting these milestones (original writings—Judean desert scrolls—Masoretes) is a long process of copying by hand. We will return to the ins-and-outs of this below. Sufficient for now is to observe that our main access to the divine deposit of Scriptures given to the covenant community in Hebrew (and some Aramaic) comes via two channels: the medieval Masoretic manuscripts—which were basically *all* we had up until the 1940s—and the scrolls found alongside the Dead Sea. It is much to be thankful for, but the numbers are still small, particularly for the periods closest to the time of writing. Fortunately, other documents may be called as witnesses to the ancient Hebrew wording.

WHAT ROLE DO ANCIENT TRANSLATIONS PLAY?

Imagine you are traveling in Spain and desperately need a quote from C.S. Lewis's *Mere Christianity*. Your English copy is back home, and all you can find is the Spanish translation, *Mero Cristianismo*. Assuming you know Spanish well and that the translation is accurate, you could make a pretty good run at approximating the English wording from the Spanish, which bears witness to the original text from which it is derived. This scenario sheds light on the role of ancient translations of the Hebrew Scriptures.

During the covenant curse of exile, many Jews began losing Hebrew in favor of the language of their foreign rulers—first Aramaic (see 2 Kgs 18:26; Isa 36:11; Neh 8:8) and then Greek. In response, major translation efforts were born. These translations of the Hebrew Scriptures not only gave non-Hebrew speaking Jews (and early Christians) God's Word in an understandable form, but they are also significant ancient witnesses to the wording of the original scriptural deposit. They join the Dead Sea Scrolls in filling the gap between the original composition and the Masoretes.

While their *Hebrew sources* have mostly been lost

(apart from the scrolls of the Dead Sea area), the resulting _translation_ documents provide a window to whatever Hebrew they had in front of them. There are five translations worth mentioning.

Greek

After the conquest of Alexander the Great (d. 323 BC), the vast majority of Jews outside Palestine (and many within) began using Greek instead of Hebrew/Aramaic. Soon a translation of their Scriptures was in order. The first major effort was the translation of the Pentateuch by bilingual Jewish scholars in Alexandria, Egypt, most likely at the request of Ptolemy II. This project was, at the time, the first major translation effort in world history! These scholars produced what is often called the 'Septuagint' (LXX for short), sometime in mid-200s BC. The prophets and psalms were most likely translated next, with the majority (though perhaps not all) of the scriptural books being translated by ~150–100s BC.

These 'Old Greek' translations were imperfect, just like modern efforts, and some are better (Genesis– Deuteronomy) than others (Isaiah, Daniel). But they were widely adopted and copied among Greek-speaking Jews and Christians. Such Greek translations are used by nearly all NT authors when they quote the OT and functioned as the 'pew Bible' of the early Christian world. Early fragments of these Greek translations survived in the Dead Sea area and in Egypt (~100 BC–200 AD). But the earliest extensive copies are the 4th–6th century AD codices Sinaiticus, Vaticanus, Alexandrinus, and Marchalianus.

The text of these 'Old Greek' translations was regularly revisited, often to bring it closer in line with the Hebrew. Decades later, after the 'parting of the ways' in the early second century, some Jews sought to produce their own Greek version because the Christians had taken over the 'Old Greek'/Septuagint. These rival Jewish translations include those of Aquila, Symmachus, and Theodotion, all completed by ~200 AD. The textual situation was so complex, in fact, that the church father Origen devoted much of his scholarly prowess to producing a massive parallel edition, known as the Hexapla (~240 AD). But even after Origen, two more revisions are attributed to Lucian and Hesychius, and in the 600s Origen's text was translated into Syriac by Paul of Tella.

There are a lot of moving parts! But while the history of copying/revising the Greek translations themselves is immensely complex, all scholars agree that they give us unparalleled insight into the wording of the Hebrew Scriptures in that important early period.

Samaritan

Though not truly a translation in the fullest sense, the Samaritan version of the Pentateuch is nevertheless distinct enough to receive attention. On the whole it is consistent with the Hebrew as we know it, though there are numerous minor differences. One of the largest is the command to build an altar on Mt. Gerizim instead of Ebal (at Deut 27:4–8), which is later reflected in John 4:20. Though the version originated before ~100 BC, we do not have any extensive copies of the Samaritan version prior to the 900s AD.

Aramaic

As mentioned above, even before the Greek era ordinary Jews were shifting to Aramaic under the occupation of the Persians. As the synagogue service began taking root, the Hebrew was read but orally translated to Aramaic so that the people could understand. By the 100s BC, some of these Aramaic translations were committed to writing in the form of a *targum* (Heb. 'translate'). For instance, a targum of Job was found among the Dead Sea Scrolls. The major Aramaic translation efforts, however, took place after 200 AD. Two were eventually sanctioned within Judaism as 'official': Targum Onqelos (of the Pentateuch) and Targum Jonathan (Prophets). Others were widely used but in an 'unofficial' capacity: Targum Neofiti, Targum Pseudo-Jonathan, Fragmentary Targum (containing excerpts), the Cairo Genizah targum, and the Writings targums. Some targums are more useful than others in shedding light on the underlying Hebrew, but they all help us understand the process by which the Hebrew Scriptures were passed on.

Latin

Around the 100s AD, as Roman influence spread, the OT

was translated into Latin. The earliest efforts are loosely called the 'Old Latin' or 'Itala,' but they were based more on the Greek than the Hebrew. However, Jerome replaced the Old Latin with his own re-translation based on the Hebrew, beginning with the psalms and then covering the whole Hebrew Bible (390–405 AD). His Vulgate—along with his commentaries comparing the Hebrew he used with the Greek to which he had access—provide yet another significant witness on the wording of the Hebrew of his day.

Syriac

Numerous early Christians spoke a form of Aramaic known as Syriac, and their ancient work translating the Hebrew Scriptures is quite important. The origin of the earliest, known as the Peshitta ('simple version'), is somewhat shrouded in mystery. It was produced at least as early as the 100s AD, if not earlier. Interestingly, many of the apocrypha were included.

Others

The five mentioned above all give direct access to some form of the Hebrew Scriptures known to the translators. There are, however, additional 'grandchildren' of the Hebrew which were largely influenced by the Greek: Coptic, Ethiopic, Armenian, Gothic, Georgian, Old Slavonic, and Arabic. These show just how far the influence of the old covenant Scriptures extended around the ancient world. But they are, at best, indirect witnesses to the Hebrew.

Each translation effort is a witness, allowing scholars to work backwards from Greek/Aramaic/etc. towards the underlying Hebrew words they used. On the whole they confirm the textual integrity of the Hebrew Scriptures over a long period of time. But they also complicate things at points. So let us turn there next.

CAN WE CONFIDENTLY RECONSTRUCT THE ORIGINAL WORDING?

The decisive US Declaration of Independence is the parchment originally signed by the members of congress on July 4, 1776 (the Matlack version). In the ensuing centuries, it has suffered significant deterioration arising from relocations during wartimes, public viewing, and so forth. In 2010 it was re-encased in argon gas to prevent further damage. If it *were* completely ruined, however, does that mean we have lost the Declaration? Of course not. We could use numerous early copies—the Dunlap and Goddard broadsides and notes from Jefferson—to reconstruct it with confidence.

The same is true for the Hebrew Scriptures, though the scale and timeframes are quite different. As outlined above, the writings originated over two millennia ago and were transmitted by hand-copying until the terminus of the Masoretic text, on which modern editions are based. Standing at the mid-way point are the manuscripts of the Judean desert and the ancient translations. From this data can we accurately reconstruct the divine deposit? We will probe two aspects of this important question.

Reconstructing the individual wording

On the whole, the Dead Sea discoveries and ancient translations have confirmed the essential accuracy of the Masoretic text and, thus, the integrity of the copying process over several centuries. For instance, the Great Isaiah Scroll, the Leviticus scroll of En Gedi, the *kaige* recension of the Greek, and Aquila's translation all reflect wording close to what became the Masoretic text— though preceding it by eight hundred years or more.

That said, any moment's reflection reveals that the process of copying ~427,000 words of the Hebrew Scriptures by hand is subject to mistakes. No scribe was perfect (even if one holds to providential guidance). Several factors can lead to erroneous wording during copying. A scribe could confuse one letter for another (ר and ד), garble the spelling, skip a word or line, or duplicate a letter or word. The Jews were famously diligent as scribes—instituting rules about spacing, column formatting, line/word-counts—but pollution still entered the stream. This is all normal for the ancient world. Several early Christian writers were well aware of OT wording variants when they interacted with the copies of Scripture available to them.

The Judean manuscripts such as the Dead Sea Scrolls, along with the early translations, provide a wealth of information to help us sort things out when questions arise about the individual wording of a passage. To illustrate, the Masoretic text may read ABD in a given verse, but a much earlier fragment from Qumran plus a surviving Greek manuscript may read ABC. In such a case, scholars engage in the work of textual criticism—a field involving the comparison of ancient manuscripts—to determine which is most likely to be the initial wording of the Hebrew. It may be that ABD arose from a slip of the stylus at some point along the way, and that ABC is superior. Such deliberations lead to the footnotes found in modern editions mentioned above. Scholars working from the Masoretic Hebrew text occasionally amend it if they believe the wording found in a Judean manuscript or ancient translation is more likely to be correct.

So how many such variations in the wording are there? Standing at the end of the process, the Masoretes themselves annotate over 1,000 possible scribal mistakes. The Dead Sea Scrolls reveal a few thousand differences in wording as well, as do the Greek translations, Samaritan Pentateuch, and others. It is difficult to quantify with precision because it depends on how you define a variation in wording, but the number on any accounting is fairly large.

However, this is no reason for alarm. All scholars admit the vast majority of variations at the individual word or phrase level are minor differences, such as spelling of names, differences in verb tense, and so forth. Few, if any, raise theological questions. And even those that may impact translation or interpretation will normally be indicated in the footnotes of modern English Bibles. Fortunately, we have a lot of data to help sort it out.

Think about it this way. It is unlikely that many of the initial words given by God have been lost altogether (Saul's age in 1 Sam 13:1 may be one of the few exceptions). Rather, we have *more* than the inspired words of Scripture. We sometimes have to sift through available alternatives in the manuscripts (i.e. ABC, ABB, ACC, BCA) to determine which Hebrew wording is best (i.e. ABC). Are there open questions? Sure. But on the whole we have high confidence that the available materials give excellent access to the 'right' Hebrew words.

Reconstructing the initial form

Oliver Twist circulates today in the form that Dickens wrote, various abridged forms, and a few movie adaptations. The story is essentially the same, but each form, or specific pattern of words in which the story is told, is distinguishable. Something like this occurs with some portions of the Hebrew textual tradition.

Though the Dead Sea discoveries and ancient translations overwhelmingly corroborate the integrity of the Masoretic tradition, in a few places they present evidence for two or more *distinct patterns of wording*, or forms of the text (beyond one-off variations mentioned above), circulating in that period. By this we mean that, for lengthier sections of the Scriptures, the Greek OT and Samaritan may share one wording pattern, some scrolls from Qumran share another, and both might differ from the final Masoretic text (as one possible example).

This plurality is often attributable to the geographic upheavals experienced by the Jews, where over time a distinctive way of transmitting a passage took hold in Egypt while another took hold in Palestine or Babylon. In many cases, we can still work backwards from these distinguishable forms and estimate the singular original from which they descended.

In other cases, the differences are more pronounced, and much research is still being done to work out the textual history. In response to this complexity, some scholars—i.e. the *Hebrew Bible: Critical Edition* sponsored by the Society of Biblical Literature—argue that, though there may have been an authorial original

Major Differences in Textual Form

Jeremiah: the main Hebrew form is about one-seventh longer and organized differently than the Greek form.

Ezekiel: an early Greek papyrus, along with some Hebrew fragments, indicate a form that is substantially shorter than that found later in the main Hebrew tradition.

1 Samuel 16–18: this section is about 45% shorter in the Greek form than in the Masoretic form.

Job and Proverbs: the relationship of the Greek translations with the Masoretic text is complex and may indicate a plurality of early forms.

Psalms: the Greek translation, Qumran versions, and Masoretic form occasionally vary in ordering/numbering and combinations of psalms.

Judges and Daniel: there are two Greek translations of these books, which in part may be due to marginally distinct forms of the Hebrew available to the translators.

of these writings, we cannot work our way back to it and should settle for multiple competing versions. I am unconvinced it is necessary to throw up our hands agnostically, simply because we do not *yet* have an airtight solution. The best course is to continue doing the hard work of taking the Masoretic Hebrew, evaluating evidence from other earlier witnesses, and making well-reasoned judgments on which wording was, so far as we can tell, originally given by God. And, to be safe, use a lot of footnotes!

SUMMARY

Antiquity has bestowed on us a treasure of ancient manuscripts of Israel's Scriptures. Of chief importance are the early and medieval Hebrew documents that give us direct access to the wording of the divine deposit, to which ancient translations (Greek, etc.) provide supporting testimony. Answering the question, 'do we have the right words of God?' is complex. And there are numerous challenging questions that will continue to keep scholars busy for years. However, if we survey the entire landscape we can answer 'yes'—with thankfulness for how God, in his sometimes mysterious providence, has preserved the *wording* of his inspired Word through the ages.

We have now covered the essentials for 'how we got the OT.' Let us explore the origins of the NT.

NT CANON:

DO WE HAVE THE RIGHT BOOKS?

Dan Brown famously puts on the lips of a character in *The Da Vinci Code*,

> The Bible, as we know it today, was collated by the pagan Roman Emperor Constantine…[He] commissioned and financed a new Bible, which omitted those gospels that spoke of Christ's human traits and embellished those gospels that made him godlike. The earlier gospels were outlawed, gathered up and burned. (pp. 231, 234)

Such claims about the NT are primarily aimed at selling books, not doing accurate history. But this notion that 'Constantine picked the books,' or 'the Council of Nicaea

In contrast to what we saw for the OT, there is no real debate among Protestantism, Roman Catholicism, and Orthodoxy on the NT: they all agree on the 27 books. The task of reconstructing the wording of these books is also quite different than that for the OT, due to a more robust inventory of early manuscripts.

picked the books,' or that anyone, for that matter, *picked the books* of the NT—and that other writings did not make the cut due to nefarious scheming—is astonishingly prevalent, even among scholars who should know better. We will see, however, that it is utterly mythical.

We will be begin, as before, with the question, do we have the 'right' books? Why these and not others? How should I think about these 'other' books that show up in the news that apparently missed the cut?

HOW DID THE NT DEPOSIT OF WRITINGS TAKE SHAPE IN THE APOSTOLIC ERA?

We pick up where we left off in Chapter 1. I argued the NT writings are documentation of the new covenant, which Jesus claimed he was inaugurating in his own blood (Luke 22:20). A few days later, prior to his ascension, Jesus asserted that the old covenant is fulfilled in two ways in the new era: his death and resurrection, and the proclamation of repentance/forgiveness to the ends of the earth (Luke 24:44–47). Christianity is, in other words, the Christ-*event* and how that event *expands the covenant community*. Jesus then charged his apostles to be 'witnesses of these things' (24:48), such that the NT took shape in a few stages between these two points.

Event

Paul famously defines the 'gospel' not as fuzzy spirituality, but as that which was 'delivered as of first importance': Jesus' death for sins, burial, and resurrection, 'in accordance with the Scriptures.' He states in no uncertain terms that if these *facts* are untrue, we should pack it up and go home (1 Cor 15:1–14). All apostolic teaching radiates from the historicity of the Christ-event (1 John 4:2; Rom 1:3–4; 1 Pet 3:18; Heb 1:3).

Eyewitnesses

If Christianity stands or falls on events in history pertaining to Jesus, then eyewitnesses are crucial. The apostolic circle 'heard…saw with their eyes…looked upon…touched' Jesus (1 John 1:1). They can confirm whether or not these *facts* are true. For good reason the apostles were extraordinarily concerned with this.

Peter argues they did not follow 'cleverly devised myths' but were 'eyewitnesses of his majesty' (2 Pet 1:16). Paul claims that resurrection can be validated by hundreds of eyewitnesses (1 Cor 15:5–8). John stresses how he was 'witness' of Jesus (John 19:35; 21:24). The eyewitness testimony of the followers of Jesus is the most important plank in their argument against opponents (Acts 2:32). Indeed, the defining feature of apostleship itself is being an eyewitness of the risen Lord (John 20:19–23; Acts 1:21–22; 1 Cor 9:1). These eyewitnesses not only passed on information about Jesus

(2 Thess 2:15; Luke 1:2; Heb 2:3), <u>but they also verified its accuracy when misinformation crept in</u> (Gal 1:8–9; 2 Cor 11:3–4; 3 John 9–12). Hence, the role of eyewitnesses in the formation of NT Scripture is essential.

Oral/written records

From the beginning, eyewitness information about Jesus' life and initial doctrinal statements were passed in oral and written form (notebooks, catechisms, liturgies). Most did not survive, but we have indications of some.

Though Paul was writing very early, he incorporates in his letters several teachings of and facts about Jesus that were circulating among the early churches before most of the Gospels were recorded (Rom 8:15 and Gal 4:6 [use of 'Abba']; Rom 12:14; 1 Cor 7:10–11; 1 Thess 5:2–4). He even quotes Jesus' words that are not found in the Gospels but were passed along orally (Acts 20:35). He also includes various creed-like passages (Phil 2:5–11; Col 1:15–20; 1 Tim 3:16) that, most scholars argue, were already in use in the earliest church.

Other 'prophecies' or 'predictions' of the apostles were circulating but not recorded explicitly (1 Tim 1:18; Jude 17–18). Luke may have kept a sailing journal during trips with Paul (the 'we' passages of Acts). It is possible that Matthew composed an initial collection of sayings 'in the Hebrew/Aramaic dialect,' as many church fathers suggest (Papias, Clement of Alexandria, Irenaeus, Origen, Eusebius, and Augustine). Among 'bookish' Christians it is no surprise that there was a lot of information sharing.

Formal NT writings

In due course, God directly inspired the writing of new covenant Scriptures, beginning with Paul, James, and Mark as the earliest writers and concluding with John, the last living apostolic eyewitness. The NT writings were written in Greek by a small number of Jewish and Gentile converts, spread across a handful of geographic locales, during a short period of time (roughly the 50s to late 90s AD). The writers knew each other at some level, and thanks to the Greco-Roman empire, the communication network among the early church was fairly efficient. Thus, even in this compressed timeframe there are signs of a burgeoning reception of new scriptural writings even within the NT itself.

What are some of the major historical differences between the formation of the OT and that of the NT?

Indications of later inspired writers acknowledging and/or using earlier inspired writings include the following:

- *Matthew and Luke* almost certainly used Mark as a source of their writings. Luke mentions prior 'narratives' to which he had access (Luke 1:1–4).
- *John* gives clear signs that he not only knew the prior three Gospels but is intentionally supplementing them (John 3:22–24 'syncs-up' with Mark 1:14–15; John 7:1–2 interlocks with the

Synoptic chronology. The recognition that John is expanding on the prior Gospels is seen as early as Clement of Alexandria).

- *Jude* appears to be familiar with *2 Peter* (or vice versa) and adopts many of its phrases often word-for-word.
- *Paul* writes in 1 Tim 5:18, 'For the Scripture says,' and quotes two passages. The first is Deut 25:4. The second, 'The laborer deserves his wages,' is a verbatim rendering of Jesus' words in Luke 10:7.
- *Peter* acknowledges Paul's letters were circulating already, which he claims some opponents 'twist... as they do the other Scriptures' (2 Pet 3:15–16). He echoes Romans in his writing of 1 Peter.
- *James* appears to be familiar with some of Paul's letters as well as Matthew's Gospel.

There is a clear pattern of inner-biblical reception just as we saw for the OT. It appears, even, that Paul declares the Gospel written by his associate Luke to be 'Scripture' (alongside Deuteronomy), and Peter in turn declares Paul's letters 'Scripture' (along side 'the others').

The NT writers were familiar with Jewish (Jude 9, 14–15) and secular writings (Acts 17:28–29; 1 Cor 15:33; Tit 1:12). They were also aware of spurious writings circulating in the early church (2 Thess 2:2; 3:17). But the consistent pattern is that the NT authors only ascribe divine authority to the OT Scriptures and, surprisingly quickly, each others' writings.

Covenant community

The collection of new covenant Scriptures took shape in short order around Jesus' gameplan of Luke 24:44–47. The four Gospels and Acts bear witness to the Christ-event (life, death, resurrection, ascension, and its aftermath). And the rest of the writings—Pauline epistles, Hebrews, 'catholic' or general epistles, and Revelation—proclaim the implications of this Christ-event, so that the community of those who repent and believe might extend to the ends of the earth. And, indeed, it has.

HOW WAS THE NT DEPOSIT RECEIVED WITHIN EARLY CHRISTIANITY?

Let us trace how the post-apostolic church acknowledged these writings as new Scriptures bearing divine authority from God. The common misconception is that the Constantine and the bishops imposed the canonical books at the Council of Nicaea (325 AD), or that Athanasius did in his *Festal Letter* of 367 AD. The former is simply false; there is no record that the scriptural books were debated at that council. The latter is a misunderstanding, as we will see below. There were no book burnings to eradicate competitors either.

So how did things really play out in the early church? We will take it in three steps (similar to our OT discussion): how the core writings were acknowledged; how the other writings were received; and how Christians indicated that they viewed them as Scripture.

You can choose your friends; you can choose, to a lesser degree, your neighbors; but you cannot choose your ancestors. They impose themselves on you without your having a say in the matter, handing down all your family history and DNA that shapes your life one way or another. The same is true for the NT writings.

Crystallizing the core writings

The early church quickly came to agreement that God gave the Gospels and the Epistles of Paul as the nucleus of new covenant Scriptures. Bishops never picked these writings or granted them canonical status. The Gospels and Paul never asked, anyhow. They simply *were*.

We will take them in turn and focus on two kinds of data: quotations/allusions (which may or may not be decisive indicators of canonical reception, as we have seen before, but they at least show the writings being *used*), and direct statements about them.

The four Gospels were acknowledged essentially from the outset. Eusebius records the early opinion that John had already sanctioned Matthew/Mark/Luke and adds his to the fourfold collection (*Hist.* 3.24.7). Hence, if anyone 'picked' the Gospels, it was John. But there is evidence beyond this. Quotations/allusions by early church writers show their use of the Gospels:

- Clement of Rome (d. 99)—quotes 'words of the Lord' found in Matthew and/or Luke, though the wording makes it hard to pin down which one (*1 Clem* 13.2–3; 15.2).
- Ignatius (d. 108)—quotes Matthew at least three

times (*Eph.* 14.2; *Smyr.* 6.1; *Poly.* 2.2) and alludes to narrative details of both Matthew (*Eph.* 19.1–2) and Luke (*Smyr.* 1.2); uses phrases only found in John (*Rom.* 0.1; 7.3; *Phil.* 7.1; 9.1).

- Polycarp (d. 155)—quotes material from the first three gospels numerous times (*Phil.* 2.3; 7.2; etc.).
- *Didache* (early second century)—cites 'the Gospel' four times (8.3; 11.4; 15.5–7). The quotation of the Lord's Prayer indicates Matthew is probably in view.
- *Barnabas* (early first century)—quotes Matt 22:14 directly (4.14).
- Celsus (ca. 160–180), an early Jewish opponent of Christianity—quotes or alludes to all four Gospels.
- Justin Martyr (d. 165)—quotes material from Matthew and Mark (*Dial.* 106.3–4), Luke (*Dial.* 103.8), and John (*1 Apol.* 61.1–4; *Dial.* 105).
- Theophilus of Antioch (ca. 180s)—quotes from Matthew, Luke, and John (*Ad. Autolycum*).

These examples suffice, for after this point quotations of the Gospels increase exponentially; Clement of Alexandria (d. 215), for instance, quotes the Gospels over one thousand times.

But quotations only tell part of the story. The early church fathers also say things *about* the four Gospels that indicate their unique authority:

- Papias (d. 130)—emphasizes that Mark wrote his Gospel based on information received from Peter (Eusebius, *Hist.* 3.39.14–16).

- Ignatius—refers to the events recorded in the Gospels as the 'inviolable archives' (*Phil.* 8.2).
- Justin Martyr—describes the Gospels as the 'memoirs of the Apostles' that 'came about by their agency,' either 'written by the apostles or their followers' (*Dial.* 103.8; *1 Apol.* 66.3).
- Tatian (d. 180)—attempts to create a 'harmony' (*Diatessaron*) out of only those deemed scriptural in his day, namely, Matthew, Mark, Luke, and John.
- *Epistula Apostolorum* (2nd century)—refers to the 'book which Jesus Christ revealed unto his disciples' containing 'the word of the Gospel'.
- Irenaeus (d. 202)—discusses at length the beauty and necessity of four, and only four, Gospels (*Haer.* 3.1.1; 3.1.2; 3.11.7; 3.11.8).
- Hippolytus of Rome (d. 236)—asserts that Christ watches over the church in the 'fourfold saving gospel' (*Comm. Dan.* 1.18.10).
- Origen (d. 254)—declares there are four and only four Gospels, though he is aware of others (*Comm. John* 1.6; *Hom. Luke*).

From the earliest period to the mid-third century, the early church was fully united around four, and only four, Gospels which they deemed to be divinely-given apostolic 'memoirs.' Indeed it was only heretical parties, such as Marcionites, Valentinians, and Ebionites, who rejected three and preferred only one—presupposing, in fact, that the four were accepted among the orthodox.

The reception of Paul's letters is also well-attested.

Various letters of Paul were quoted—explicitly or via clear allusions—by Clement of Rome, Ignatius, Polycarp, Irenaeus, and Tertullian. True, some fathers like Justin Martyr did not explicitly cite Paul's letters, but on the whole the evidence is extensive.

There is also early confirmation of 2 Pet 3:15–16 regarding a corpus of Paul's letters circulating *together* at an early stage. For instance, Polycarp commends the Philippians to 'study carefully' the letters of Paul (*Phil.* 3.2), and Ignatius urges the church at Ephesus to remember Paul, 'who in every letter remembers you' (*Eph.* 12.2). Irenaeus commends them as fully authoritative, asserting that the 'words of the Lord are numerous' and can be found both in the gospels as well as in 'the epistles of the blessed apostle' (*Haer.* 4.41.4).

From the earliest days, then, the indisputable core of the NT consisted of the Gospels and Paul. Even the early heretic Marcion reflects this structure with his 'mutilated' NT consisting of a shortened Luke and a modified collection of Paul's letters.

Clarifying the rest of the writings

But what about the rest of the apostolic writings beyond Paul? They were included in this two-fold collection very early. Origen writes that the 'texture of the net [of Scripture] has been completed in the Gospels and in the words of Christ through the Apostles' (*Comm. Matt.* 10.12), and even earlier Ignatius and Hippolytus assert that the two-fold source of authority in the church is the 'gospel' and 'apostles.' But the details for each of the other books is case specific, with some facing more debate than others.

Acts, due to its association with the Gospel written by Luke, was accepted very early (Irenaeus, *Haer.* 3.14.1; *Anti-Marcionite Prologue to Luke*; Clement of Alexandria, *Strom.* 5.12). First Peter was rarely doubted, and numerous early church fathers quote it (Polycarp, Irenaeus, and Clement of Alexandria). Similarly 1 John was recognized very early to have come from the apostle John and, thus, was rarely in doubt; it is quoted by Polycarp and Irenaeus, among others.

The remainder—Hebrews, 2 Peter, James, 2–3 John, Jude, and Revelation—are often listed among the 'disputed'/'debated' books by church fathers like Eusebius and Origen. Dispute, however, has no bearing on the intrinsic scriptural quality of the writing; it merely indicates that some parts of the church took a while to *recognize* that quality. Though there were— and still are—debates about the identity of the author of Hebrews, it typically traveled with Paul's letters in early manuscripts and was quoted as early as Polycarp. Second Peter is first mentioned explicitly by Origen, who quotes it several times while acknowledging that some have their doubts. James and the other shorter epistles were not quoted extensively in the second century, and Eusebius classifies them as 'disputed writings, which are nevertheless recognized by many' (*Hist.* 3.25.3; Origen treats them similarly). Revelation was debated due to its eschatological content. But Justin Martyr, only a few decades after its composition, commends the prophecy (*Dial.* 81.4), and Irenaeus quotes it numerous times.

The ups-and-downs these writings faced is not terribly surprising, any more than it was for some of the OT writings. But even as *some* books on the margins were debated by *some* parts of the church for *some* period of time, the evidence is clear that there was widespread agreement on a stable collection of writings received as Scripture given by God. And by the mid-fourth century, the 27 new covenant writings are fully acknowledged, specifically in Athanasius' *Festal Letter* of 367. The letter is remarkably instructive, when one looks not simply at the book-list but also how his explanation for *why*:

> Since some have taken in hand to set in order for themselves the so-called apocrypha and to mingle them with *the God-inspired scripture*, concerning which *we have attained to a sure persuasion*, according to what the original *eyewitnesses* and ministers of the word have *delivered unto our fathers*, I also… have decided to set forth in order the writings that have been put in the canon, *that have been handed down and confirmed as divine*…[He lists all 27 books accepted today]…These are the springs of salvation.

Note the phrasing highlighted. Athanasius is not 'choosing' these 27-books, but acknowledging how the church has become persuaded they are God-inspired, scriptural, delivered by eyewitnesses, handed down, and confirmed as divine.

Signaling the writings received as divinely authoritative

Very early the church used NT writings in worship. Justin Martyr, for instance, writes that, when Christians in a region gathered on Sunday, 'the memoirs of the apostles or the writings of the prophets are read' and expounded, followed by prayer, the Lord's Supper, and offerings (*1 Apol.* 67).

Collecting writings into larger codices (bound books)—e.g., the 2- and 4-gospel codex (p45, p75), the Pauline codex (p46), the 'Apostolos' codex (p74)—also conveys how they functioned as Scripture. Individual writings were not just random letters or stories sent to a small group of people but inherently *belonged* together, which is how covenant documentation works. And in some sense we could say that codex=canon, at least for the group that assembled the codex, since book covers by definition rule things 'in' or 'out.' However, we should recall the distinction from Chapter 1 that 'canon' determined by one particular group is distinct from 'Scripture,' which is determined by God. For example, Codex Sinaiticus (4th century) and Codex Alexandrinus (5th century) include all 27 books—but Sinaiticus also includes *Barnabas* and portions of *Shepherd of Hermas*, while Alexandrinus includes *1–2 Clement*. These extra inclusions may have been considered divinely-given Scripture by the maker of each codex, but perhaps they were just 'nice-to-have'.

A final indication of reception of the NT are the various 'canon lists' produced from the early 200s onward, where various writers set forth by name the books used as Scripture. I will tabulate them using a Y when there is agreement with the 27-book collection, – where a book is excluded, and * where a book is 'disputed.'

	Gospels-Acts	Paul+ Hebrews	General epistles	Revelation
Muratorian Fragment (2nd–4th century)	Y	– Hebrews	– James – 1–2 Pet – 3 John	Y
Origen (Eusebius, Hist. 6.25; Comm. John 5; Hom. Josh 7.1)	Y	Y	Y	Y
Eusebius (Hist. 3.3.5; 3.25.1–7)	Y	Y	James*, 2 Pet*, 2–3 John*, Jude*	Y
Clermont List (~300–350)	Y	Y	Y	Y
Cyril of Jerusalem (Catech. 4.36)	Y	Y	Y	–
Mommsen List (~359)	Y	– Hebrews	– James – Jude	Y
Athanasius (367)	Y	Y	Y	Y
Epiphanius (Pan. 76.22.5)	Y	Y	Y	Y
Apostolic Canons 85 (ca. 380)	Y	Y	Y	–
Gregory of Nazianzus (Carm. 12.31)	Y	Y	Y	–
Jerome, Augustine, Rufinus	Y	Y	Y	Y

These lists elaborate on what we observed above: the Gospels and Paul were the stable core, but some other writings (Hebrews, some of the general epistles, and Revelation) were subject to debate. Athanasius did not end the debate—further indication that he was not imposing a decision on the worldwide church—but the trajectory is clearly from more debate to less over time. At the Synods of Hippo (393) and Carthage (397), the earliest ecclesiastical councils to discuss canon, only the 27 books were discussed.

In short, there is strong attestation of a core scriptural collection (Gospels and Paul) from the earliest days, and around this nucleus the remaining inspired writings orbited—though it may have taken a while to reach full consensus. There were, however, 'other' books beyond the 27 that received some attention.

WHAT ABOUT ALL THESE OTHER BOOKS?

Movies like to play on the trope of the slightly quirky uncle that shows up once or twice a year at big family gatherings, bears some sort of family resemblance, but no one is really sure that he is actually part of the family or not. He either *is* or *is not*—but sometimes it is hard to know whether to claim him as our own and give him a seat at the table.

This kind of scenario somewhat captures what went on in the early church regarding 'other' books beyond the 27 given by God as new covenant Scripture. The situation is somewhat complex, though not nearly as convoluted as what we saw on the OT side for the apocrypha. We will first discuss those books that were given at least some serious consideration in various quarters of the church, followed by those indubitably rejected as spurious.

Debated writings

A handful of early writings were sometimes quoted (in ways indistinguishable from scriptural writings) or even included among 'canon lists.' These writings were often well-known in parts of the early church, and on the whole their content, apart from a few quibbles, are basically orthodox. Let us mention a few key ones.

1 Clement (late 1st century) is an epistle written by Clement of Rome to the church. It is quoted by Irenaeus and Origen and included in the *Apostolic Canons*, Codex Alexandrinus, and Papyrus 6.

The *Didache* (early 2nd century) is an early treatise on Christian living. Clement of Alexandria makes reference to it, Eusebius includes it among the 'rejected' books (*Hist.* 3.25.4), and Athanasius commends it as useful for instruction, though non-canonical.

Barnabas (early 2nd century) is a treatise on the relationship between Christianity and Judaism. Clement of Alexandria quotes from it frequently, and Origen even refers to it as 'the catholic epistle of Barnabas' (*Cels.* 1.63); as mentioned above, it was included in Codex Sinaiticus. But Eusebius labels it 'rejected'.

The so-called *Gospel of Peter* (early 2nd century) only survives in fragments dealing with the passion of Christ. Origen refers to it (*Comm. Matt.* 10.17), but Serapion (ca. 180), though at first allowing it to be read, eventually condemned it due to its heterodox content and false attribution to Peter (Eusebius, *Hist.* 6.12.2).

The *Shepherd of Hermas* (mid-2nd century) is an enigmatic collection of visions and parables. Irenaeus quotes it with 'as the Scripture declared' (*Haer.* 4.20.2), and the Clermont List as well as Codex Sinaiticus include it. However, the Muratorian Fragment declares it can be read privately but not in worship (as does Athanasius), and Eusebius labels it 'rejected.'

Other writings such as the *Gospel of the Hebrews*, *Gospel of the Egyptians*, *Acts of Paul*, *Acts of Andrew*, and *Apocalypse of Peter* received some attention, such as scattered quotations (e.g., Clement of Alexandria) or inclusion in one-off canon lists. But Eusebius gives the majority opinion that they are 'disputed' or 'rejected' (*Hist.* 3.25.5–7).

These writings, to the extent they have survived, provide insight into the beliefs and practice of the early church. They were, and still can be, read with profit by the church. But there is scant evidence they were ever used in worship, and apart from an opinion to the contrary here and there, the early church never recognized them as given by God to be new covenant Scripture.

Gnostic writings and other apocryphal literature

Recent decades have seen growing fascination about another category of writings from the first centuries after Christ. These writings cover various themes and were more like 'fan-fiction' about Jesus. They were never given serious consideration by the church as *Scripture*, though sometimes quoted or read. Most give 'secret revelations' about Jesus (from which *apocrypha* is derived). While some are mentioned in the early church (e.g. the *Gospel of Thomas*, *Gospel of the Ebionites*, and *Gospel of Truth)*, many were otherwise unattested until the discovery of the gnostic codices at Nag Hammadi, Egypt (1945).

Essentially all of these focus on secret knowledge and fail altogether to bear the imprint shared by all NT Scripture: namely, a focus on the Christ-event (death for sins, resurrection, ascension) and its transforming power (faith/repentance/forgiveness) in the life of the worldwide covenant community. No wonder, then, that the orthodox church never acknowledged them as bearing the true witness of the apostolic circle, regardless of their clever names.

A Sampling of 'fan-fiction' about Jesus: The Gospel of Thomas gives 114 'sayings' (logia) of Jesus, which at times overlap with Luke. The Gospel of Judas and Apocryphon of John both arise from Sethian gnosticism and focus on secret (and clearly heretical) wisdom from Jesus. The Protevangelium of James expands on the infancy narratives of Matthew/Luke with a particular focus on Mary. The Infancy Gospel of Thomas does likewise but instead focuses on the wizard-like exploits of Jesus as he grew up. And the Gospel of Mary presents Mary Magdalene giving Peter secret knowledge she got from Jesus.

SUMMARY

Before his ascension, Jesus invested his apostles with the authority to be 'witnesses' to two things: his own life, death, and resurrection that consummated the old covenant and inaugurated the new; and the proclamation of repentance for the forgiveness of sins to the ends of the earth. This happened orally at first, but fairly quickly the apostles and their close associates (like Mark and Luke) set forth in writing the divine deposit. They recognized the divine marks in each others' writings, and passed them down to the early church. At points there was debate about whether to receive some of them (Hebrews, some of the general epistles, Revelation) as divine Scripture. And in some circles other books like the *Didache* or *Shepherd* were in the mix. But consistently we see the church gravitating towards the twenty-seven 'that have been handed down and confirmed as divine' (Athanasius). No one chose them. They chose themselves.

But do we have accurate access to the *words* of these books? We turn there next.

What if we found one of Paul's 'other' letters mentioned in 1–2 Corinthians? Should we put it in our Bibles?'

This is a tantalizing question. But if Scripture is what we have defined it thus far, the answer seems fairly straightforward. A writing is not Scripture—and thus rightfully included in our biblical canon—simply because an apostle wrote it. Something is Scripture if it is inspired, deposited in writing, received as divinely authoritative, and intended by God to function as covenant documentation. Paul no doubt wrote a lot more than the ~2,000 verses we have, but not everything would be inspired (e.g., a letter to his mother). The 'missing' letters were not apparently ascribed divine authority, though the 'severe' letter produced results (2 Cor 7:8–9). Most tellingly, such letters do not appear to have been intended as permanent written documentation for the covenant community, for God did not see fit to preserve them in his church. They are not even mentioned outside Paul's own writings. Thus, on balance, it is safe to say that we indeed have the 'right' books. None are missing, and none need to be added—even if we found a lost letter of Paul.

5

NT TEXT:

DO WE HAVE THE RIGHT WORDS?

Bart Ehrman, one-time religion chair at the University of North Carolina at Chapel Hill, is famous for making statements like this:

> Interpreters of the NT are faced with a discomforting reality that many of them would like to ignore. In many instances, we don't know what the authors of the NT actually wrote. ... In point of fact, many interpreters, perhaps most, *do* ignore it, pretending that the textual basis of the Christian Scriptures is secure, when unhappily, it is not.

'Text and Interpretation,' *TC* (2010)

He elaborates on such sentiments in his popular books, such as *Misquoting Jesus* and *The Orthodox Corruption of Scripture*. His claim is that, in short, 'no, we do not have the right words' of the NT.

Modern Muslim apologists make similar claims. The Islamic doctrine of *tahrif al-nass*—that Jews and Christians have intentionally corrupted the text of Scripture—is loosely rooted in Qur'an 2:75, 5:13, and 5:41, though it was more clearly developed by later writers such as al-Mahdi, Ibn Qutayba, and Ibn Kathir. The basic claim is that the wording of the NT has been distorted, modified, or even lost due to nefarious scribal activity; for this reason, the claim goes, the NT does not mention Muhammad, among other things.

There would be no such skepticism, of course, if we had the original NT artifacts—the material and inked words—produced by the inspired writers. However, none of those survived. But has the *wording* inspired by God survived? Or has it been corrupted or even lost?

A brief glance at a modern English version of the NT may fuel these concerns. The very first page of Matthew in the ESV, for instance, mentions competing spelling of names, or that 'some manuscripts' say something else or 'omit' phrases. Several verses at the end of Mark are introduced with a foreboding comment about how the 'earliest manuscripts' lack the subsequent verses, which are marked off with [[...]]. Much like for the OT, the footnotes of even the most streamlined copy of the ESV, NIV, and other translations mention variant wording quite often. How do we account for all this? We will first look at where our English versions of the NT come from, then examine the early manuscript evidence for the wording of the NT.

WHERE DOES OUR ENGLISH BIBLE COME FROM?

Every major translation of the NT comes directly from one of two main editions of the ancient Greek. The KJV/ NKJV uses one of the revised editions of Desiderius Erasmus's first modern printing of the Greek NT (1516), earning the label *Textus Receptus* by Elzevir in 1633. Most others, such as the ESV, NIV, NASB, use the *Novum Testamentum Graece* (26th-28th edition), which shares the same text the UBS *Greek New Testament*. (We will later deal with the differences between the *Textus Receptus* and the *Novum Testamentum Graece*.)

Where, then, do these printed editions get their Greek wording?

HOW DO WE ACCESS
THE SCRIPTURAL DEPOSIT IN GREEK?

Both printed editions (and all others) arrive at their text through consulting a treasure of ancient manuscripts. At present, ~5,500 individual *Greek NT* manuscripts have been catalogued (by a research team in Münster, Germany). It is challenging to be precise with the number, for some manuscripts registered separately may actually be part of the same manuscript (double-counting), some are catalogued but then lost, and so forth. Yet this number is generally sound (it is sometimes overstated as ~5,700). It is a wealth of data—far more than what we have for the OT. Let us examine a few different angles on the data.

Kinds of manuscripts

The earliest, and often most interesting, are the papyri, which are manuscripts written on material made from the stalks of the papyrus plant. This material is not very durable, so the vast majority of the ~130 NT papyri (at present) are fragmentary; some contain only a few words or verses, while others are more intact. Most were written in upper-case (uncial) letters without spaces between words and generally without punctuation and accents.

Though papyrus continued being used for several centuries, around the 300s–400s some Christian scribes began shifting from papyrus to more durable (but more expensive) material made from animal skins, known as parchment or vellum. The earliest stage of these parchments (fourth to ninth centuries) were also written in upper-case letters and are called majuscules. They have survived far more intact; most contain a sub-collection (Gospels, Pauline epistles, etc.) but a few contain the entire NT. At present there are roughly ~260–280 majuscules (over 300 are catalogued, but some are missing or double-counted).

Around the 800s–900s, a revolution in Greek handwriting took place from upper-case to cursive script, and scribes copying the NT followed suit. These later manuscripts, called minuscules, were copied on parchment or paper and constitute the vast majority of what has been preserved—well over ~2,700. Related to them are ~2,400 lectionaries, which derive from the same era but are excerpts of NT passages used in worship services, rather than continuous copies of the text. Even smaller portions of the Greek NT circulated as amulets (talismans containing citations of the NT), ostraca (broken pottery used for writing material), and inscriptions.

Dates of manuscripts

Assigning dates to manuscripts, particularly if the scribe left no indication, involves the study of handwriting, ink, materials, and other features. We cannot be overly precise in dating many manuscripts, particularly older ones. However, with reasonable estimates of dates, we can say that solid numbers of Greek manuscripts have survived in every century from the third through the fifteenth (after which we enter the printing press era).

Two are dated to the second century, but none so far are confirmed to be from the first century. Around 20% of known manuscripts are from the first millennium, and the remainder are post-1000. This imbalance is due to the higher likelihood of deterioration of older manuscripts; the tendency for scribes to destroy their exemplar (the manuscript they are copying from) once they have finished copying it; and the rise of monastic copying centers in the medieval era.

Contents of manuscripts

The manuscripts that make up this large number do not all comprise the whole NT. In fact, only around sixty do. The rest include one book or a sub-collection of books; and even then, many times a given book may be only partially attested due to deterioration or lost pages. Thus, the frequency with which each of the 27 NT books shows up in the pool of manuscripts varies considerably. The Gospels are the most well-attested, followed by Paul, Acts/general epistles, and Revelation. But even within these categories there is variability. For instance, among the papyri we find only 2 fragmentary portions of Mark compared to 19 of John, and 1 of Galatians and Colossians compared to 5 of Romans.

Quality of manuscripts

It becomes clear from the preceding discussions that, while all ancient manuscripts certainly have market and museum value, they are not all equal in value for studying the Greek text. This is further compounded by the quality of the scribe who made the copy, as well as the quality of the exemplar being used. Some scribes were incredibly diligent, even reproducing the column width, erasures, gaps, and obvious errors from the exemplar. But if the exemplar itself is mediocre, the scribe's output is mediocre as well despite his precision. Alternatively, the exemplar could wonderfully preserve an ancient and accurate text, but the scribe using it could be sloppy.

In this way, an ancient manuscript (say, from the fourth century) could be medium quality, while a much later manuscript (say, from the fifteenth century) could be high quality. Earlier is not always better, and later is not always worse. Scholars working with these manuscripts have to take a lot more into consideration than the type and estimated date of a manuscript.

In sum, we have an embarrassment of riches in terms of Greek NT manuscripts, including abundant attestation of all 27 books in the Greek manuscript tradition, and for that we are very grateful. These manuscripts provide us with the primary access we have to the words inspired by God. But, as with the OT, ancient translations also help.

Reflecting on the NT Manuscripts

We should be careful to avoid misconstruing the large number of manuscripts (e.g., in apologetics). Not all the ~5,500 are papyri or elegant majuscules (only a few); not all are early (the lion's share are not); not all contain the complete NT (only ~1% do) or even complete copies of what they do contain (most of the early ones are highly fragmentary); and not all are of the same quality.

WHAT ROLE DO ANCIENT TRANSLATIONS PLAY?

The spread of Christianity throughout the Roman empire brought the NT scriptures into contact with non-Greek speakers and, thus, the need for translation. In our study of the Hebrew Scriptures, such translations play a major role in bearing witness to the inspired Hebrew; the same is true for the NT, but to a lesser degree owing to the larger repository of Greek manuscripts available.

The most important translation efforts are Latin, Syriac, and Coptic.

The oldest is the 'Old Latin,' originating in the second century. It has no official edition but shows up in a variety of manuscripts (even as late as the medieval period). It was eventually replaced by Jerome's Vulgate. There are thousands of surviving Latin manuscripts.

Next in line are the series of Syriac (a dialect of Aramaic) translations: the 'Old Syriac' of the 3rd/4th century; the Peshitta of the 4th/5th (the standard edition for the Syrian church); the Philoxenian produced in 507/508; and the Harklean produced in 615/616. Each provides varying levels of insight into the early Greek text. Over 300 Syriac manuscripts have survived.

A collection of Coptic translation efforts, beginning in the 3rd century, are also important for the study of the NT text—particularly those in the Sahidic and Bohairic dialects. Several hundred Coptic manuscripts have survived.

Other early translations efforts—though leaving abundant manuscript remains—are relatively less important due to their later dates and mixed quality: Ethiopic, Georgian, Armenian, Gothic, and Old Slavonic.

These efforts also provide a useful window into the state of the Greek text in the early centuries, where, as mentioned above, our extant Greek manuscripts are less plentiful than in later eras. Most of the time they *confirm* the wording already found in this or that Greek manuscript. However, in very rare instances NT scholars have hypothesized that the authentic wording is found *only* in one of these translations and has been lost in the Greek tradition. A well-known example is 2 Pet 3:10, where the editors of the *Novum Testamentum Graece* now argue that the 'right' word at the end of the verse is found only in Syriac and Coptic, not in any surviving Greek manuscripts.

But how do scholars make such decisions? With what degree of confidence can we take all these Greek manuscripts as well as translations and work our way back to the wording given by God to the NT authors? In how many places do the manuscripts disagree, anyhow?

CAN WE CONFIDENTLY RECONSTRUCT THE ORIGINAL WORDING?

500,000, give or take.

That is the most recent—and most accurate—estimate of the number of variations in wording (other than trivial differences in spelling and the like) found in the known Greek manuscripts of the NT.

It is a somewhat shocking number, especially given that the number of words in the Greek NT is ~138,000. If there are so many variations, how do we know we have the 'right' wording? We will break down this question into two parts: the process of reconstructing the wording,

The number of variations in wording increases with the number of copying events. Since we have so many manuscripts, we have a lot of variations.

and indications of the integrity of the wording as it has been passed down.

Reconstructing the individual wording

As with the Hebrew Scriptures, the tedious process of copying the NT by hand among thousands of manuscripts discussed above was imperfect. Variations in wording enter the copying process in one of two ways. Scribes sometimes make unintentional errors: skip a word or line, duplicate a word, misspell a word, garble the lettering, confuse a note in the margins (from a prior scribe) as part of the text, and so forth. The vast majority of mistakes in copying are of this sort.

Scribes sometimes make intentional modifications as well. They may spot an error in the manuscript from which they are copying and attempt to correct it. They may try to 'harmonize' a passage in the gospels with a parallel version in another gospel. They may tweak an OT quotation to match the wording they are more familiar with. Few such changes were theologically-motivated but, rather, were attempts to fix things—though sometimes their cure was worse than the disease!

Most variations are small, involving an average of ~2 words, according to recent calculations. While many are insignificant ('Jesus Christ' vs. 'Christ Jesus'), many can

Some scholars tend to exaggerate the theologically-motivated 'corruptions,' but more recent research on scribal habits has shown that most such changes fit with normal patterns we would expect.

be exegetically significant ('let us have peace with God' vs. 'we have peace with God' at Rom 5:1). A handful of somewhat lengthy and well-known variations generate heated arguments—Mark 16:9–20 (endings of Mark); John 7:53–8:11 (woman caught in adultery); John 5:3–4 (angel at the pool); Acts 8:37 (the eunuch's confession of faith); 1 John 5:7–8 (the three witnesses in heaven); and others—but these are more the exceptions than the norm.

Thus, the seemingly ghastly number of variations mentioned above is not that surprising. If, over time, you have thousands of scribes copying tens of thousands of words, the opportunities for scribal mistakes run into the millions! In fact, some short phrases in the Greek NT have dozens of known variations while others (so far as we know) have zero. This explains how you can have more actual variations in wording than total words.

So what do we do with all this mess? That is where the field of NT textual criticism enters in. Scholars compare the wording among these manuscripts and, where there are variations, make educated judgments about which wording is likely to be correct. They consider external and internal evidence. External evidence deals with the specific manuscripts: which ones say ABC vs. CBA vs. any other alternatives, and how much weight do we assign to that? Internal evidence focuses on hypothesizing how the variations in wording may have come about through scribal activity, and which wording best fits the author of the given NT book being studied. To illustrate, if a critic were faced with AABC and ABC as the two known options for a given portion of the NT, he/she might conclude that the latter is correct and the former came about through accidental repetition, even if AABC is found in some otherwise 'good' manuscripts.

A 'critical edition' of the Greek NT is comprised of the outcome of such decisions across the full text. Editors present what they believe to be the best reconstruction of the wording and provide footnotes ('apparatus') containing alternative wordings which they evaluated but ruled out. There are, of course, open questions in various places, but these efforts to reconstruct the text have attained a remarkable level of stability.

The *Textus Receptus* mentioned earlier derives from Erasmus' consultation of a small number of medieval manuscripts. *Novum Testamentum Graece* traces its origins to the late 1800s, when two Cambridge scholars (Westcott and Hort) replaced the *Textus Receptus* with their own edition that incorporated numerically more and far older manuscripts. Their work has been revised over the past decades to the most current edition.

Westcott and Hort believed they had, for all practical purposes, achieved the goal of reconstructing *the* 'original' wording given to the NT authors. Some recent scholars have slightly moderated this optimism and prefer to speak of an 'initial' text instead of 'original,' arguing that we can only go back to the mid-second century and no further. However, many still believe we can make the inductive step from the second century and (acknowledging some open questions) treat the reconstruction as, for all practical purposes, the authorial 'original.' Let us examine reasons for this confidence.

Indications of integrity

First, recent data confirm the substantial stability of the textual tradition over time, despite the plethora of scribal errors (see Point of Interest below).

Second, we can look at scribal habits. The common misconception is that early Christian scribes were a sloppy, unprofessional bunch. This may be true for some, particularly for manuscripts that were copied for personal use rather than church use. However, we can point to several lines of evidence that suggest a higher degree of professionalism than often granted.

Recent Research on the Integrity of the NT Text

Based on the 2013-2017 revised editions of Acts and General Epistles.

Non-variation: Approximately 15% of the text has no known variations.

Stable core: Among the sixteen most important manuscripts spanning a ~1,000 year period, the wording is fully identical ~70% of the time.

Agreement of polar opposites: For various reasons, the wording found in Novum Testamentum Graece is, from a text-critical perspective, deemed by most scholars to be the polar opposite of that represented by the Textus Receptus. They are, on average, the most different in their wording. But even then, they fully agree with each other ~94% of the time!

Chief representative: The reconstructed text in Novum Testamentum Graece is attested by the famous (and arguably best) fourth-century Codex Vaticanus at a rate of 96% agreement.

Early text in later manuscripts: Several manuscripts copied after 1100 AD contain wording that closely matches that found in much earlier manuscripts, even papyri over a millennium older. This suggests a high degree of diligence in copying, as well as the availability of older manuscripts to later scribes.

Essentially all Christian manuscripts, from the earliest period, used a system of abbreviations for sacred words like God, Lord, Christ, and so forth—called *nomina sacra*. We are not fully sure what prompted this practice (perhaps the treatment of YHWH inherited from Jews), but it took hold immediately and across geographic regions. Similarly, the preponderance of NT manuscripts, from the earliest days, were copied in codex (book) form rather than scroll form. This may have been due to the desire to combine writings into larger collections (like the four Gospels). There also is evidence that the practice of numbering NT paragraphs within manuscripts, once thought to be a later innovation, could go back as early as the second or early third century. Furthermore, similar types of annotations (paragraph indicators, markings for OT quotations, etc.) appear across a variety of manuscripts from a very early period. None of these 'paratextual' features were imposed by anyone; they basically appeared overnight. This suggests a fairly high level of coordination, information sharing, and so forth among the early scribes.

We also see various signs that the scribes were well-engaged in their work, even the medieval scribes who are often accused of being somewhat mindless in their copying. For instance, some scribes include marginal notes describing how they compared their exemplar

While it is true that some manuscripts were copied informally, often for private reading, many if not most appear to have been copied by scribes with some level of training.

against earlier, better manuscripts; how they were aware of what this or that church father said about the wording of a specific passage and took that into consideration; and so forth. Some scribes use various in-line notations (ancient equivalents of insertions) to indicate awareness of alternative wording in the passage they are copying. In short, they were pre-modern textual critics.

Were any of the scribes perfect? Of course not. However, when we take into consideration the whole picture of the process of transmitting the text by hand from its point of origin to the late Middle Ages, we attain tremendous confidence not only that we *can* reconstruct the Greek wording inspired by God—but that, in essence, we *have*.

SUMMARY

So let us return to where we started this chapter. For Ehrman (who is not alone), the lack of the autographical artifacts, combined with the large number of variations in wording found in the manuscripts, means we have no idea what words the NT authors wrote. I hope this chapter has shown that this is a gross exaggeration. Are there open questions? Of course. The process by which the inspired words have been handed down—though providentially guided—was still subject to the fallibility of human scribes. However, we have very high confidence in the integrity of the text. For good reason, then, one of the world's foremost textual critics (who co-edits *Novum Testamentum Graece*) has recently concluded: 'the high

Two additional statistics indicate we should have high confidence in the NT. The text of the most recent critical edition of Acts/General Epistles agrees fully with all four major majuscules (the ones that are highest overall quality) for 78.3% of the words; and it agrees with at least one of them literally 99.9% of the time. This is remarkable support for our reconstructed text in the best manuscripts.

agreement rates connecting these witnesses demonstrates that a large body of text was safely transmitted from the very beginning of its transmission through the Byzantine period to today' (Klaus Wachtel, 2017).

What about the Muslim critique of *tahrif al-nass*? The Qur'an regularly commands Muslims to consult the *Injil* (gospel) to check Muhammad's message (3:3–4, 45–50; 5:46–47; 10:94). Thus, in Muhammad's day (600s AD), the NT to which he had access was apparently deemed trustworthy by Allah. So when did Christians allegedly pull off this massive corruption of the NT? If before the 600s, then there is no reason for Allah to commend something that was already corrupted. (This would also call into question the integrity of Allah's revelation as a whole.) If after, then the critique is irrelevant. Why? Because all Christian Bibles use manuscripts dating well before the 600s! Even if massive corruptions entered the textual stream after the time of Muhammad (which is doubtful anyhow), they do not matter because textual critics weed them out to reconstruct the pre-600s wording. Indeed, it is rather surprising that Muslim apologists would cling to this critique at all, for it is so easily defeated.

6

CLOSING THOUGHTS

We have reached the end of our journey through the past few millennia, tracing how God has graciously condescended to reveal himself in words, given under inspiration of his Spirit, to men who set them forth in writing as documentation of his gracious covenant—which were then passed down and received as divinely authoritative. It is a beautiful, though at times complex picture.

I will not belabor such a short volume by rehashing all the data. Instead, I will wrap up with a handful of essential 'talking-points' that can help Christians clarify their own understanding of, and confidence in, the process by which we got the Bible.

We should be clear on what Scripture is in the first place. It is not an arbitrary collection of human devotional writings that was made into canon by later Jewish and Christian leaders. Rather, it *the inspired deposit of writings received as divinely authoritative for the covenant community.* Scripture imposes itself by virtue of what it *is.* Canon, then, is the output of a process of recognition or reception of these writings, and only these writings, by the people of God.

We should have confidence that we do have the 'right' OT books. The threefold Hebrew Scriptures—Torah, Prophets, Writings—are the divine deposit given by God. They bear witness to this within themselves, and early Jews and Christians (including Jesus) were very clear on this from the earliest days. The acknowledgement of the 39 (or 24, by Jewish counting) books comprising this deposit took time, given they were composed over a thousand-year period. The apocrypha were debated, but the strongest case can be made, following Jerome and the Reformers, that they are secondary and edifying, but not covenant Scriptures bearing divine authority.

We should have confidence that we have the 'right' words of the OT. We access the wording of these Hebrew Scriptures using a combination of medieval manuscripts, the scrolls of the Judean desert, and ancient translations that bear witness to the earliest text.

We should have confidence that we do have the 'right' NT books. The nucleus of the new covenant Scriptures—Gospels and Paul's letters—was received very early. The rest of the writings comprising the 27-book collection, though debated at the margins, gravitated towards this nucleus and received widespread acceptance within the first centuries.

We should have confidence that we do have the 'right' words of the NT. We are blessed with a wealth of high-quality Greek manuscripts conveying to us the authentic wording. The large number of variations in wording arises from the staggering number of copying events (thousands of scribes copying tens of thousands of words). But diligent textual criticism allows us to use all this data to reconstruct the wording with high reliability.

How did we get the Bible? The answer to this question driving this book is clear. 'Men spoke from God as they were carried along by the Holy Spirit,' and the written deposit has been transmitted in the covenant community with high integrity, by the providence of God, ever since.

Through these Scriptures, we are all, now, witnesses of these things: Christ suffered and died and on the third day rose again, so that repentance and the forgiveness of sins may be proclaimed to all the nations.

FURTHER READING

Endnotes have been avoided to make this text as readable as possible. My focus, at any rate, has been on the primary sources from Judaism and early Christianity. I am indebted, of course, to a wealth of writings on canon and text. The works used—which I would commend to the reader for further study (though I do not agree with all of them)—are included below, arranged by chapter. All of them have influenced my thinking for Chapter 1, so I will focus on the other four.

CHAPTER 2

Beckwith, Roger. *The Old Testament Canon of the New Testament Church and Its Background in Early Judaism.* Grand Rapids: Wm. B. Eerdmans, 1985.

Brueggemann, Walter. *An Introduction to the Old*

Testament: The Canon and Christian Imagination. Louisville, KY: Westminster John Knox, 2003.

Carr, David. *The Formation of the Hebrew Bible: A New Reconstruction.* Oxford: Oxford University Press, 2011.

Chapman, Stephen B. *The Law and the Prophets: A Study in Old Testament Canon Formation.* Forschungen zum Alten Testament 27. Tübingen: Mohr Siebeck, 2000.

deSilva, David A. *Introducing the Apocrypha: Message, Context, and Significance.* Grand Rapids: Baker Academic, 2002.

Ellis, E. Earle. *The Old Testament in Early Christianity: Canon and Interpretation in the Light of Modern Research.* Grand Rapids: Baker Books, 1992.

Lim, Timothy H. *The Formation of the Jewish Canon.* Anchor Yale Bible Reference Library. New Haven: Yale University Press, 2013.

McDonald, Lee Martin. *The Formation of Biblical Canon. Volume 1. The Old Testament: Its Authority and Canonicity.* London: Bloomsbury, 2017.

CHAPTER 3

Brotzman, Ellis R. *Old Testament Textual Criticism: A Practical Introduction.* Grand Rapids: Baker Academic, 1994.

Hengel, Martin. *The Septuagint as Christian Scripture: Its Prehistory and the Problem of Its Canon.* Translated by

Mark E. Bidde. Old Testament Studies. Edinburgh: T&T Clark, 2002.

Kaiser, Walter C. *The Old Testament Documents: Are they Reliable and Relevant?* IVP Academic, 2001.

Tov, Emanuel. *The Greek and Hebrew Bible: Collected Essays on the Septuagint.* VTSup 72. Leiden: Brill, 1999.

VanderKam, James C. *The Dead Sea Scrolls Today.* 2 ed. Grand Rapids: William B. Eerdmans Pub. Co, 2010.

CHAPTER 4

Blomberg, Craig. *Can We Still Believe the Bible? An Evangelical Engagement with Contemporary Questions.* Grand Rapids: Brazos, 2014.

Bruce, F. F. *The Canon of Scripture.* Downers Grove, IL: IVP Academic, 1988.

Gallagher, Edmon L., and John D. Meade. *The Biblical Canon Lists from Early Christianity: Texts and Analysis.* Oxford: Oxford University Press, 2018.

Head, Peter. *How the New Testament Came Together.* Cambridge: Grove, 2009.

Hill, Charles E. *Who Chose the Gospels? Probing the Great Gospel Conspiracy.* Oxford: Oxford University Press, 2010.

Kruger, Michael J. *Canon Revisited : Establishing the*

Origins and Authority of the New Testament Books.
Wheaton: Crossway, 2012.

———. *Question of Canon: Challenging the Status Quo in the New Testament Debate.* Downers Grove, IL: InterVarsity Press, 2013.

McDonald, Lee Martin. *The Formation of Biblical Canon. Volume 2. The New Testament: Its Authority and Canonicity.* London: Bloomsbury, 2017.

Metzger, Bruce M. *The Canon of the New Testament: Its Origin, Development, and Significance.* Oxford: Oxford University Press, 1997.

CHAPTER 5

Bruce, F. F. *The New Testament Documents: Are They Reliable?* Grand Rapids: Wm. B. Eerdmans, 2003.

Gurry, Peter J. 'The Number of Variants in the Greek New Testament: A Proposed Estimate.' *New Testament Studies* 62/1 (2016): 97–121.

Gurry, Peter J. and Elijah Hixson (eds.). *Myths and Mistakes in New Testament Textual Criticism.* Downers Grove, IL: IVP Academic, *forthcoming.*

Hurtado, Larry W. *The Earliest Christian Artifacts: Manuscripts and Christian Origins.* Grand Rapids: Wm. B. Eerdmans, 2006.

Lanier, Gregory R. 'Dating Myths: When Later

Manuscripts Are Better Manuscripts,' in Gurry/Hixson, *Myths and Mistakes*.

———. 'Quantifying New Testament Textual Variants: Key Witnesses in Acts and the Catholic Letters.' *New Testament Studies* (2018).

———. 'Taking Inventory on the 'Age of the Minuscules': Later Manuscripts and the Byzantine Tradition within the Field of Textual Criticism.' *Currents in Biblical Research* 16/3 (2018): 263–308.

Porter, Stanley E. *How We Got the New Testament: Text, Transmission, Translation*. Grand Rapids: Baker Academic, 2013.

Wachtel, Klaus. 'On the Relationship of the 'Western Text' and the Byzantine Tradition of Acts — A Plea Against the Text-Type Concept.' Pages 137–48 in *Novum Testamentum Graecum: Editio Critica Maior, III/3: Studien*. Editors Holger Strutwolf et al. Stuttgart: Deutsche Bibelgesellschaft, 2017.

BAPTISM

The Water That Unites

BEING MADE
RIGHT WITH GOD

Understanding Justification

GOOD WORKS
AND REWARDS

In this Life and the Next

GROWING IN HOLINESS

Understanding Sanctification

JESUS CHRIST

LOVING THE
OLD TESTAMENT

One Book, One God, One Story
FOREWORD BY TIM KELLER

MARY

Mother of God?

PAPACY

Its origin and role in the 21st century

SUFFERING

How God Shapes Us through Pain and Tragedy

Christian Focus Publications

Our mission statement –

STAYING FAITHFUL

In dependence upon God we seek to impact the world
through literature faithful to His infallible Word, the Bible.
Our aim is to ensure that the Lord Jesus Christ is presented
as the only hope to obtain forgiveness of sin, live a useful life
and look forward to heaven with Him.

Our books are published in four imprints:

CHRISTIAN
FOCUS

Popular works including biographies, commentaries, basic
doc-trine and Christian living.

CHRISTIAN
HERITAGE

Books representing some of the
best material from the rich heri-
tage of the church.

MENTOR

Books written at a level suitable
for Bible College and seminary
students, pastors, and other serious readers. The imprint includes
commentaries, doctrinal studies,
examination of current issues and
church history.

CF4•K

Children's books for quality Bible
teaching and for all age groups:
Sunday school curriculum, puzzle
and activity books; personal and family devotional titles, biographies and
inspirational stories – because you
are never too young to know Jesus!

Christian Focus Publications Ltd,
Geanies House, Fearn, Ross-shire,
IV20 1TW, Scotland, United Kingdom.
www.christianfocus.com